RIDING THE SHOW-RING HUNTER

Jane Marshall Dillon

Bill Weikel, Editor
THE FARNAM HORSE LIBRARY

HORSE LIBRARY

The Farnam Horse Library
8701 North 29th Street
Omaha, Nebraska 68112

FRONT COVER
Riding a show-ring hunter would be an absolutely unforgettable event on a hunter of this caliber. Photographed by A. W. Fretz, Newark, Delaware. The name of this obviously capable rider is unknown.

PHOTOGRAPH ACKNOWLEDGMENTS:
Loudoun Hunt Horse Show, Leesburg, Virginia; Jane Marshall Dillon, Vienna, Virginia; Junior Equitation School, Vienna, Virginia, Full Cry Farm, Vienna, Virginia; Howard O. Allen, Allen Studio, Middleburg, Virginia; Theodore Cogswell, Staff Photographer, Farnam Companies, Inc.

No portion of the text or illustrations of this book may be copied or reproduced in any manner whatsoever, in whole or in part, without express written authorization in advance from the publisher, The Farnam Horse Library.

PRINTED IN U.S.A.
Copyright 1972
JULY 1972
SECOND EDITION

CONTENTS

1 What Is A Hunter? 4

2 How To Make Sure That You Don't Get Asked Back To Hunt (And Vice Versa) 13

3 Getting Yourself And Your Horse Turned Out For The Hunter Show 22

4 Win Your "Under Saddle" Class! 28

5 What Happens At A Walk, Trot And Canter And At Their Variations? 33

6 "Big Time" Hunter & Jumper Courses 42

7 Riding A Simple Hunter Course 46

8 Know The Rules Of The Game You Play 52

9 Judging Hunter Classes — Performance And Horsemanship 57

INTRODUCTION

RIDING THE SHOW-RING HUNTER

A strange thing has happened in the United States in the last half century. In the early 1900's it seemed as if the horseless carriage was going to do away with the horse! And for a while, as the motor driven monsters increased, the horse really did seem doomed to disappear from the scene. And then this strange thing began to happen. As we became more mechanized as a nation, we began to long more ardently for some of our links with the world of nature and of animals. Most of all, one large, frequently beautiful and generally amiable animal spelled enchantment for countless thousands. This could be none other than THE HORSE!

More and more city dwellers, who could afford the luxury, began to drive their cars out to the country, there to ride their horses. Those who could not afford to own horses flocked to schools or stables for lessons or just to rent horses. Even this rented horse could carry the rider through the park on a sunny fall day and transport him out of his world of city streets and apartments. There is an indefinable quality about this particular relationship that seems to inspire a very special sense of well-being.

Horse fever has seized the nation and seems to be gaining momentum with every passing month. In some areas, stables, large or small, sprout out of every suitable—and sometimes unsuitable—piece of ground. In certain suburbs, almost every home that boasts one or two acres will have a small barn within view of the back kitchen windows. On weekends, the highways will be alive with horse trailers and vans, en route to the weekly shows. In fact, the fascination of this sport has become so great that each of several horse shows, held in the same vicinity and on the same day, may be jammed with entries!

The variety of ways in which people can now enjoy "the sport of kings" is almost endless in its diversity and subsequent specialization. This booklet will deal with only one segment of the horse world—that of the hunter, and in particular the show ring hunter, in the United States today.

CHAPTER ONE

WHAT IS A HUNTER?

A newcomer to your area, who has lived all her life in a big city and whose family has recently bought country property in any of the eastern states where horses, and in particular hunters, form a very natural part of life, might astound you with the questions: "What precisely *is* a hunter? I don't know much about them, so I would like some proof that I am paying for a bona fide hunter. Should I demand 'papers' similar to those that a friend received when he bought a thoroughbred? Another thing that confuses me is the fact that I saw a book called 'Training Hunters, Jumpers and Hacks.' Someone else told me that all hunters must be able to jump, or you couldn't even compete in hunter classes at most horse shows. But if hunters are really jumpers, can they be registered both ways, and why is there a distinction made? Are hunters and jumpers two different breeds or are they the same breed? And what exactly are hacks?"

To the individual who was reared in what we term "hunt country" or anywhere near it, and who had the faintest interest in horses, these questions may sound positively absurd, and yet they are perfectly normal and sensible from the uninitiated. Sometimes the simplest questions are the most difficult to answer. In the same way we might find ourselves struggling to simplify the answer if someone asked us "what is a sports car?" To answer our *un*-horse oriented friend, we had best start at the beginning.

First of all, hunters are not a breed. *Breeds* can be established only as the result of the ability of a particular type to reproduce offspring that will have the same general *physical* characteristics. Generally in each breed there have been "foundation sires" that have transmitted certain qualities to their "get" to a marked degree. In establishing a breed, meticulous records are kept over a period of time. When recognition as a breed is accorded, records will be kept in that particular association's "Stud Book," and the names and forebears of all "registered" animals of that particular breed can be found there. Many established breeds are relatively old, while recognition of new breeds is constantly sought. Thus we find horses registered as Arabians, Thoroughbreds, Clydesdales, Percherons, Standardbreds, Morgans, American Saddle Horses, Quarter Horses, to mention just a few. But nowhere in the United States do we find a *breed* in which your hunter can be registered as a hunter! The same thing holds true for ponies. We find registrations for Welsh, Connemara, Hackney, Dartmoor, Shetland and a horde of lesser known breeds. No matter if you foxhunt regularly on a large pony, all of whose forebears for several generations have been tremendously capable pony hunters, you still cannot register your pony hunter as a "pony hunter" in *breed* classification. For horse show purposes, in the case of both horses and ponies, you will register in the hunter division, but this has nothing to do with breed.

The term "hunter" refers to the particular job that is expected of that horse or pony, not to his ancestry. Thus, your hunter may be a Thoroughbred or he may not; he may be a Connemara pony or he may be "cross-bred" in a great variety of ways. Naturally, certain types that seem the most successful at the job that they must do have created a certain image for most of us as to what a hunter should look like.

What *should* a hunter look like? In the horse world as well as in other areas, form (that is conformation or body build) should be related to *function;* in fact it should be the direct result of function. So suppose we consider what we expect the hunter to do. We will consider first the original role of the hunter—which is to serve as a "suitable mount to hounds" for the sport of foxhunting.

In essence, he must be able to carry his rider safely across country of various types and degrees of ruggedness safely and comfortably. Since he may be put to this work for quite a few hours, he should use up as little energy as possible with each stride. So instead of wasting his strength with high, short steps, we would like to see him move with long, low effortless strides that cover the ground with the minimum output of effort. In hunter circles, this is part of what is termed "good movement." In addition, this animal must be able to jump safely the normal height of fences or obstacles (some will be natural, some man-made) which he finds in his path.

Of course this is oversimplifying the picture. We expect many other qualities in our hunters. We expect them to be of reasonably calm temperaments; we do not want them to become so carried away by the stimulation of galloping with a group of horses that we find ourselves outdistancing the field master! We expect our hunters to be agile and clever, so that they will be able to cope with the fallen logs, steep stream banks and uneven terrain that they will encounter. We expect them to be fairly bold in facing strange sights and smells. These might include a pen full of squealing pigs, a clothesline flapping in the breeze, a funny looking little bridge, an odd looking piece of equipment—the good hunter cannot afford to panic. Besides all the sterling qualities that we have just mentioned, we count on a few more yet. This bold, calm, clever, efficiently

A well constructed, working hunter of the type you might see in an actual foxhunt.

moving creature must be "pleasant in company." Lashing out at another horse or even worse, kicking at a hound, are crimes of the first order! Besides all this, the hunter must be agreeable to the wishes of his rider, no matter how much these may differ from his own! And last, but by no means least, his way of going (gaits) and style of jumping should be comfortable from the point of view of the human on his back. All this is quite a lot to ask for (or to find, for that matter!) in one package, but it is precisely what we expect from our field hunter, whether horse or pony.

Foxhunting on horseback is quite an old sport. In our own country, in the days of George Washington, almost every member of the "landed gentry" supported a pack of foxhounds and enjoyed a rather informal version of foxhunting. But much of our open country, suitable for foxhunting, is no longer very open. Houses and entire developments mushroom up, devouring more and more of our good hunt territories. As a result of this, several rather radical changes have come about.

The first, I believe, is the fact that members cherish their existing hunts more devotedly than ever. They may have to trailer their mounts fifty miles instead of "hacking over" to a neighbor's farm, but hunt they will. In the early twentieth century "turn out" (that is, equipment, grooming and attire) became somewhat more formal than it had been in the early years of our country. From that point on, unlike most aspects of dress which have become increasingly casual in America, hunt attire and turn out have remained *essentially* the same. Inevitably there are minor changes, but within my own memory (a matter of the past forty years) it is quite astounding to realize how slight these are by comparison with styles in general! I suspect that this is all part of that basic longing to preserve what aspects we can of our country heritage and our relationship with the soil, seasons, animals, woods and wildlife.

Secondly, as we have less and less open country and more and more people who want to enjoy their "hunters," another aspect of the sport has assumed great importance and popularity. This is the "Hunter Show" with perhaps half a dozen different divisions and an even greater diversity of classes. Here the situation may become positively bewildering to the innocent spectator, visiting in the nation's capital, for example, who chances to buy tickets to The Washington International Horse Show. As he looks over his show catalogue, scattered among a generous assortment of events for International Jumpers, American Saddlebreds, and Arabians, he will come upon a wide variety of classes all bearing the word "hunter" in some part of the caption. We will mention the most important and should note that even these do not comprise a complete list of *all* the hunter divisions which you may find at horse shows throughout the country. Studying the events scheduled for the week-long show in Washington, the following will be included: Green Conformation Hunters; Working Hunters, Appointments; Green Working Hunter Stake, 1st year; Amateur-Owner Hunters Under Saddle; Conformation Hunter, Model; Small Pony Conformation Hunter Under Saddle; Large Pony Working Hunter Stake; Small Junior Working Hunter, Appointments. Each of the classes mentioned belongs to a different hunter division; each division will have four or five of such classes; each will lead to an individual championship! This great diversity of classes gives us a clue as to the tremendous interest and degree of specialization in just one aspect of the world of horses in our country today!

Are we still talking about that bold, athletic, calm and agreeable animal that must take care of himself and his rider across country, in all weathers and over all sorts of terrain? Not exactly, although originally these same horses competed at the annual country horse shows. As the ratio between horse shows and hunts changed in the direction of more and more shows, the typical show ring hunter began to become more and more differentiated from his blood brother, the field hunter. Brilliance becomes more important than calmness. Meeting every fence from an ideal line of take-off becomes more important than the ability to carry the rider safely over uneven ground and unexpected obstacles. Finally, the fit, muscular animal whose overall appearance is quite appropriate for the hunt field may look altogether out of place at the big horse show.

Exactly the same thing has happened in the case of the true (field) hunting pony and the show ring hunter pony. So we might say that our hunters could be grouped into four *general* categories (with numerous sub-groupings) as follows: Field hunters and show ring hunters, pony field hunters and pony show ring hunters. Normally, when you use the word "hunter" you are talking about a horse as opposed to a pony; otherwise, you will hear the word "pony" added to the descriptive term. Undoubtedly, it may come as a surprise to people from some sections of this country to discover that large—and occasionally even small—ponies frequently make superb hunters both in the hunt field and in the horse show ring. Many, but not all, of these hunter ponies are cross-bred and carry some horse blood in their veins. Whether cross-bred or of pure "pony" breeding, this smaller animal seems to retain a certain initiative and ability to cope that we may have bred out of our horses. This quite possibly could be as a result of the much longer period in which humans have made every decision for the domesticated horse. Added to this, we cannot overlook the effect of the race horse industry, which is interested in selective breeding for speed first and foremost. At the same time that the life of the horse becomes more sheltered, ponies still roam in almost complete freedom in some parts of the world. Even in this country, on large pony breeding farms, ponies may be left to shift for themselves to a much greater degree than would ever be permitted the thoroughbred horse. The effect of this seems to be all to the good for the pony and for the small human who rides him.

Thus far, we have discussed what we expect in general terms of several categories of hunters. We also mentioned that since an animal becomes a hunter as a result of what he *does* rather than who he is, so to speak, we could not have precise breed specifications. At the same time, what he does will be much limited, or enhanced, by the way in which he is put together. So there is definitely a body style that can very appropriately be termed "hunter type."

Let us think of what physical equipment the hunter will need for his particular way of life. He will need stamina for long hunting days. So he must have a deep enough chest to amply accommodate a big heart and lungs. A narrow weedy animal will not be a good stayer. But he must be a good galloping type too. This means that he should not be as wide and blocky as a draft horse, with bunchy as opposed to long "running" muscles. And he must be clever and athletic. So we will avoid an animal that is so short in the back that he will lack suppleness, or so long in the back that he is structurally weak. We will also want to avoid the animal with a short, blocky neck; he will not be very maneuverable. We must give particular attention to his primary traveling gear—his feet and legs. If excessively slender they will not support the heavier mass of the body plus the weight of the rider. Horsemen speak of a horse not having enough bone, which means precisely the same thing. Viewed from the front, legs should be columns without deviations that will put undue strain on bones, tendons, ligaments and muscles; joints should be prominent enough to provide good points of attachment for muscles and ligaments. Feet should be of sufficient size to support the body. An attractive, if not gorgeous, head is a very pleasant asset.

In general, we seem to be describing an animal of good quality, somewhat more substantial in appearance than the racing type of thoroughbred, but considerably finer than the draft horse.

In actual hunting, as you look around you, while the majority of mounts in the field will probably be "good hunting type" (that is, look like Thoroughbreds with quite a lot of substance, or half-breds with some Thoroughbred blood), you may see a few animals who look rather coarse, or quite rough and rangy, and who still do an adequate job. If a horse hunts well, many faults of conformation will be overlooked.

What about the show ring hunter—how will his appearance differ? Theoretically, it *need* not differ at all in "Working Hunter" divisions, although with the increasingly keen competition at big horse shows, even the entries in the "working hunter" classes are likely to be very impressive and "breedy" in appearance. When you consider the "Conformation Hunter" division, where body build counts a definite percentage, the more nearly the horse is a "model," the better the chances of winning the class. As showing becomes more and more competitive, a few paradoxes seem to develop. A conformation horse that is considered in show condition not only must have a bloom on his coat and be immaculately turned out, but fashion now decrees that he should be almost rolling fat. It is doubtful that he would last long on a strenuous hunt, but it is unlikely that his owner will take this animal out hunting anyway. An injury could end his career in the conformation hunter ranks.

Are we overlooking that smaller version of a hunter that was mentioned earlier with such enthusiasm? Not in the least; he can come under our scrutiny right now! Ponies up and down the east coast of the United States have multiplied in truly astounding numbers. Not only the quantity but the quality has vastly changed. You will still see the "backyard variety" in abundance—the short coupled, rough coated, somewhat coarse version that those who are unfamiliar with ponies may imagine typical. On the other hand, the number of very attractive ponies that one finds in the hunt field or at small horse shows indicates the trend. And when you reach the big horse show, you have a real eye opener. Frequently the largest division in the entire show will be the "Pony Hunter." And even so, many times the show had to utilize a numerical shut off point to limit entries. Here, at the big show, you will see truly beautiful ponies of hunter type, who perform brilliantly over fences.

These ponies have been "bred up" until many are positively elegant in appearance. Frequently this has been accomplished by crossing with horses, most notably Arabs and Thoroughbreds. The resulting progeny seem to retain those intrinsic "pony" characteristics of self-reliance and ability to go pretty much anywhere and over anything that they want. The average pony outjumps the average horse in comparison to his size to an extent that is downright embarrassing to the horse owner. Normally, ponies learn as much in one year as horses learn in two. Apparently, there is a tacit admission of this fact in the horse world. Horses are given two "green" years to jump fences at lower than standard heights in the working hunter division. Hunter ponies are permitted one "green" year only, and even during that one year they jump fences at the regular height for their division!

A very natural question at this point might be, "If a pony mare is bred to a Thoroughbred stallion, is their offspring still a pony?" As in most matters, there has to be an arbitrary ruling to avoid dispute. In this case, he is a pony if at maturity he measures no more than 14 hands and 2 inches at the withers (a hand is four inches); if he is an eighth of an inch over that size, he must be classified as a horse!

Even the pure pony—no admixture of horse blood—many times hunts well in the field, and with true pony self-assurance, may also compete brilliantly in the show ring. In fact, it is not unheard of to take the conformation pony out to foxhunt—something that is rare indeed in the case of the conformation horse.

Now suppose we consider the question that related to jumpers. Here again we are describing *what* the horse does rather than his ancestry. It is true that in a hunter class, the horse jumps; however, it is not designated as a "jumper" class. You will probably hear it referred to as an "over fences" class. In watching the hunter "over fences" his style, manners and pace all are considered. Fences will not be raised to determine the winner. In judging a jumper class, the horse may behave like a true demon as long as he proceeds forward and clears the prescribed course of jumps. In fact, the greatest crowd pleaser in the jumper ranks may be the horse that kicks back at the apex of his fences and throws in some sizeable bucks between! Scoring is done on an arbitrary basis of numerical penalties for faults incurred at fences (i.e., knock-downs, refusals, etc.). The only other faults considered are for loss of forward motion and fall of horse and/or rider. Jumps may be raised to determine the winner; or, in successive jump-offs, time may become the deciding factor, between clean rounds, or rounds having the same number of faults.

Obviously, then, jumpers cannot be considered a breed either. In fact, the differences in ancestry of the jumper are considerably greater than

The versatile pony hunter. This 14h.2" cross bred pony has been at the top in show ring competition for many years. In the off season, she has been an excellent field hunter.

in the case of the hunter. Hunters do conform to a general type. The same thing is not necessarily true of the jumper. While the ideal now for big competition in the jumper world seems to be the Thoroughbred, there are so many exceptions that exceptions almost become the rule! I have known of "Saddle Horses" that were famous jumpers. Occasionally, you find chunky "cold blooded" types that amaze the public with their ability to bounce over big fences. Not infrequently, jumpers emerge from the ranks of hunters. Hackney ponies, cross-bred with all sorts of horses, have produced some remarkable jumpers. The same thing may be true of a Clydesdale cross. And perhaps most surprising of all is the fact that, to my own knowledge, at least three ponies have outjumped their larger competitors in "big time" competition. One of them, Stroller, of the British Jumping Team, is well known to the horse show world today, having outjumped everything in Europe in various competitions more than once.

The word "hacks" has many meanings. Primarily it refers to a horse used for riding on the flat as opposed to over fences.

So jumpers could also be hunters (though probably not very good ones in the hunt field) and hunters could be jumpers; occasionally you find horses and also ponies who successfully compete in both divisions at horse shows. Up to a certain point, their training, ideally, should follow just about the same path.

What about "hacks?" This is a word of many meanings. Primarily it refers to a horse used for riding on the flat as opposed to over fences. However, you are said to hack your horse to the hunt meet when you ride him there, even though this did include jumping a few fences. There are many varieties of "hack" classes in horse shows; the term is sometimes used synonymously with "under saddle." In the event of a tie for championship in a hunter division, you will be told to get ready to "hack off" the tie. This means that you will be asked to walk, trot and canter and perhaps to gallop, but not to jump. So as you see, while the term is used in several different ways, it relates to the animal used for general riding, or the *act* of general riding, mostly without jumping. ■

CHAPTER TWO

HOW TO MAKE SURE THAT YOU DON'T GET ASKED BACK TO HUNT (AND VICE VERSA)

Even though the show ring hunter seems to have seized the center of the stage, his original role was quite different. Where there is still enough open country to make it possible, there are areas in which, throughout the hunt season, the real highlight of the week lies in the hunting mornings. Ardent followers of the chase will endure practically any hardships in order to rise in the grey dawn and meet with friends to enjoy this fundamentally satisfying, age-old game.

We will not consider foxhunting in any depth in this booklet. Volumes abound and can be found in any public library which describe every phase of the topic. However, those who are interested in hunters in any form will want at least a superficial acquaintance with the conventions of the foxhunting world. Practically everything that you do in show ring hunter competition has its roots in field hunting. We will introduce you to the sport through a somewhat unique—we hope—account of a hunting incident.

The M. F. H. (Master of Fox Hounds) of one small, conservative hunt, had an amazingly funny story to tell in connection with an uninvited guest who simply appeared at one of their fall meets. There really are so many lessons to be learned as to WHAT NOT TO DO that it's worth recounting. A gentleman whom we will call Mr. X arrived, dressed to the teeth, in hunting pink and riding a very poorly schooled stallion. (Yes, we really do mean stallion.) His horse not only refused every fence and got in everyone's way but he charged around, under such poor control, that he was a positive menace to the entire field. In fact there was hardly a hunting sin that he and his owner did not commit. He managed to step on a hound and to ram into other horses. He made a constant racket and rustling during checks when the huntsman was attempting to listen. The day was a real disaster from the point of view of people who like to foxhunt. Luckily, the kindly M. F. H. had a wonderful sense of humor and his version was rather like that of a Hollywood comedy. Apparently at one point the day was enlivened, if not by being able to stay with hounds, by watching Mr. X's fiery steed roll with him in a cold New England stream. When Mr. X managed to drag himself and his horse to the bank, it was noted that the seat of his white breeches was covered with yellow oil. Apparently he was hunting in a new saddle that had been oiled so recently that it had not dried. The "end of day" notes were heard rather early when it was obvious that there would be no "traditional" sport that day! Members thanked the M. F. H. for the day's sport (with a bit of a twinkle in a good many eyes) and started to hack back to the original meeting place. At this point, the M. F. H. managed to get the hunt secretary aside and asked that he ride in with Mr. X, and try in casual conversation, to clue him in a bit as to usual hunt etiquette. But this tactful effort totally backfired. "What do you mean?" retorted Mr. X, in reply to the suggestion that his stallion was a bit too green and not exactly a "suitable conveyance after hounds." "This is potentially the best piece of hunting horseflesh in the field today." There are several equally incredible sequels to this account, but they are not really pertinent. What *is* pertinent is the fact that the hunt secretary had no choice but to write to Mr. X to explain to him some of the normal hunting amenities and to regret that they could not invite him to join them out hunting. This actually happened, and amongst a group of very friendly, hospitable people who would have been glad to have Mr. X hunt with them under different circumstances.

What particular lessons might you, as a newcomer to the area, learn from this account? First of all, arrange for an invitation to come out and hunt before you appear. Don't plan to hunt until you ride well enough and your horse is schooled well enough to insure that you will not get in the way of others. Don't plan to hunt a stallion, under normal circumstances. Occasionally you find stallions that are so well mannered that they cause no problems in the field, but these are the rare exceptions. Don't appear in "pink" (actually scarlet) unless and until, after several years, you have been invited to wear the colors of the hunt. However, after you have been "awarded your colors" it is appropriate to wear your scarlet jacket on regular days with your own or with other hunts. (The reference to scarlet applies to gentlemen; ladies generally continue to wear black—more about this later.)

If you have the bad luck to get a refusal at a fence, don't block the way for others; get out of the way by circling to the back before you try again.

Don't let your horse kick or step on a hound or kick at or bump others in the field.

Don't come out in tack so new that it advertises its newness by oil coming off on your clothing.

This rather informal way of describing a bizarre hunting incident may not have clarified the foxhunting picture for you, but at least it may have dramatized a few "faux pas" to avoid. Now, let's present the positive.

Correct attire for a guest planning to hunt as she prepares to leave for the day's excitement. The Dalmatian was left at home, of course.

Hunts are not like the movies; you don't just pay and attend, nor do you "crash the party." They are privately supported and one must be invited to join, or come out on a "cap fee." However, it is quite all right to let the word get around that you would like an invitation to hunt—assuming that you have an appropriate mount and ride sufficiently well, and that you and your horse will be properly turned out.

What is proper turn out? Custom varies a bit from hunt to hunt and sometimes varies in the same hunt on week days as opposed to Saturdays or holiday meets. Your best bet is to ask advice from a member. If for any reason this isn't feasible, the following advice will see you through without embarrassment. If you are an adult, you should wear a black bowler —derby to most of us—and it should have an attachment called a "hat guard" on it fastened to a ring in the back of your hunt jacket. (Instead of a bowler, children in the hunt field normally wear black velvet hunt caps.) Your jacket should be of a winter weight woolen material; again you can feel safe in black or charcoal. You will wear a riding shirt of the neck band variety, so that you will have something to fasten your stock to. The stock is plain white and needs only to be tied in a square knot and then secured by a plain "gold" stock pin, worn horizontally. The regular stock pin looks very similar to a safety pin and sometimes goes by that name. If the prospect of tying your stock throws you into a panic, buy a ready tied one, but in any case tighten it until it will not gap at the neck and be sure to fasten it in front to the shirt button, or it will almost certainly twist around and "ride up." At this point I might add that if it is a bitter day and you are afraid that you will be cold, wear a soft snugly fitting sweater under your shirt or an undershirt cut in such a way that it will not cause bulk at the neck and spoil the neat appearance of your stock. Anyway, you will be wearing a yellow woolen vest, which will probably keep you warm enough. Tuck the ends of your stock into the vest so that they cannot flap around; it is a good idea to pin them to your shirt, underneath the vest. Well-fitting buff or brown woolen breeches are always acceptable. Plain black boots that look as tall and slender as possible complete the essentials. If your horse is sluggish, wear hunting spurs. If you have one, and know how to manage it, carry a regulation hunt whip. Normally you will wear pigskin or similar leather gloves. The preceding is the simplest description of attire that will get you by, until you learn the details of the preference of a particular hunt. For example, some hunts feel that it is appropriate to appear in "ratcatcher" (informal attire, generally tweeds and brown boots, etc.) on week days; some do not. In any and all cases, avoid appearing in sleazy-looking clothes for hunting; bright yellow, lightweight cotton breeches cannot fail to look garish, for instance.

In the American Horse Shows Association Rule Book that comes out annually, you will find a complete description of correct attire for individuals of each sex and under different conditions. It would be a good idea to study this carefully. In case you cannot locate this or a similar reference book, perhaps a few more details as to appropriate dress would help.

You hear of "winning your colors." Each hunt selects a certain "hunt livery." This refers to the color of the collar and the particular emblem on the hunt buttons. Only members who have hunted competently and courteously for a prescribed length of time are invited to wear the hunt buttons and colors. Ladies or children normally continue to wear their black hunting jackets and have the buttons and collar changed. Under the same circumstances, gentlemen wear scarlet coats with the hunt collar and buttons; in this case, breeches will be of heavy white twill. Scarlet is normally worn by all members of the hunt staff.

Who do we mean when we speak of the "hunt staff?" This is the group of individuals who are responsible for handling the actual foxhunting aspects of a hunt. (A hunt has considerable business and social obligations to handle in addition to the sport of hunting. The president of the hunt will be the chief business executive, but he is not necessarily a member of the actual foxhunting staff.) In the field of hunting, the Master of Foxhounds (the M. F. H.) is in charge. He may hunt the hounds himself, or there may be a huntsman, either professional or honorary, who occupies this post. To assist the huntsman and the M. F. H. there will be two or more "whippers-in" (whips) who also may be either professional or honorary. The other member of the hunt staff is the Field Master. When there is a Field Master, members of the "field" (everyone else out for the sport of following hounds) may not pass him at any time—unless for unusual reasons they are directed to do so. Sometimes the M. F. H. will double as Field Master himself; you do not ride past him.

Professional huntsmen or whips are employees of the hunt as opposed to being members. The ribbons on the back of their hunting caps (which, incidentally, are normally worn only by members of the staff and children in the hunt field) are worn hanging down by professionals and up by others.

Years ago, when I was beginning to hunt, and knew very little about it, I decided that it would be a good idea not to pass anyone in scarlet, unless specifically invited to ride on up, and it wasn't a bad deduction! About the same time, I figured that any of these same gentlemen would probably be good guides to follow so that I would not get lost or separated from the main part of the field. This works out well most of the time, too.

Incidentally, before we entirely abandon the matter of hunt attire, one more point needs clarification. The terms pink and scarlet have been bandied about, but the word "red" never appears. This is just one more peculiarity of the foxhunting world. Don't say that you met a man in a

The hunt is shown moving off in a typical foxhunting area. Many horsemen are working hard to keep alive the magic of the hunt, and to foster the interest of young riders so that they, too, can perpetuate the tradition of this thrilling sport.

red coat; instead you use the terms "hunting pink" or scarlet.

Next, let us consider how your horse will be dressed. First and foremost, he must be *clean*. This admonition is heard so often that it would seem superfluous. Unfortunately, this doesn't seem to be the case. Getting your horse scrupulously clean, particularly if you have no horse vacuum, really is no easy task. Most horses that hunt are clipped, which does make grooming easier. Unless a horse is kept quite heavily blanketed and has a very fine coat in addition, you almost have to clip for hunting. Otherwise, the horse gets very hot and wet on warm days or if you have any sort of fast run. Not only does his coat look rough and unattractive when wet, but he can easily get a bad cold or even pneumonia, if not very, very carefully cooled out. So the best bet is to go ahead and clip. On this, the amateur will need professional help, certainly for the first time or two. But once the horse is clipped, you do have to be quite careful about putting him out in the paddocks on cold windy days. (It isn't exactly ideal to turn the horse out in his blanket, but sometimes it is the only solution for short periods during the day. He will probably need an additional blanket at night, when standing in his stall.)

In addition to having a clean horse, you want to be sure that his chin whiskers and the hair up the back of his legs are trimmed and that his mane is pulled to the length of about five or six inches. Mane and tail should be very carefully brushed out, until every little hair is separated. In some hunts it is customary to braid the manes and tails for holiday meets; some braid on weekends, too. (See page 24 for a description of braiding.) Here, one must find out the custom of that particular hunt; it is as embarrassing to be overdressed as underdressed.

The decision as to what to wear will be easier in the case of the horse than the rider. If the horse goes kindly and stays under control in a snaffle, this is ideal. If there is a chance that he may get a bit "strong" in the snaffle, a short shank Pelham is probably the next best bet. The "full bridle" that was much used a generation or two ago has largely disappeared. Any standard hunting (flat) saddle—almost always "forward seat" now—of good quality will be appropriate. You will see a number of hunting saddles with suede inserts on the flaps. They hold up better than one would expect, and do create a nice snug frictional contact of leg to saddle. A threefold leather girth is adequate and correct. If you are riding a very round-barreled horse, you may need a breastplate to keep the saddle in place. The breastplate provides a nice addition to your hunting gear in any case. And if your horse needs it, you can always add the martingale attachment. One more very nice little extra is the hunt flask for gentlemen and the sandwich case for ladies and children. A little brandy or sherry comes in extremely well during a long check, after a few hours out in the cold!

One final word before we leave the topic of turnout. Without belaboring the point, I would like to say once again that all equipment should be thoroughly *clean.* Your saddle, bridle and breastplate or martingale should be soft and shining from having had a good saddle soap worked into it. Bits, stirrup irons and spurs should be sparkling clean too. Any good metal polish will do the trick.

The other things that you need to know to get off to a good start are mostly just a matter of nice manners and consideration of others. Simply behave the same way that you would if you were a guest under any other circumstances. The M. F. H. is your particular host (or hostess, as the case may be) so when you arrive be sure that you greet him—or her. If you are hunting as the guest of a member, you will have no financial responsibilities. If you have asked permission to come out on a "cap fee" arrangement, seek out the hunt secretary, introduce yourself and pay the fee then and there. If you are alone, fall in towards the back of the field, unless specifically invited "to come on up." In most hunts, especially

Typical of the young and green hunter prospect. This filly has not yet learned to properly estimate the amount of effort needed for the particular fence. With experience she will use herself more economically.

small ones, the regular members seem to have their special niches, and generally prefer to keep it that way.

If you are hunting in an area where there are narrow panels (chicken coops, lower sections of fence, logs cemented into stone walls, etc.) the field may pile up a bit in front of them. Don't start for that particular panel until the way is clear. If your horse should refuse, don't block the way for others. Get out of the way as quickly as possible and start again from the back.

Gates that were closed and have been opened must be reclosed. However, as a newcomer or a guest in the field, this responsibility is unlikely to fall to you.

Keep quiet during "checks" if the huntsman is attempting to listen.

Stay at a safe distance from the rump of any horse that you don't know—in fact, we might say of any horse at all. If members of the staff or others double back, turn your horse's head towards them; this can

It isn't necessary to understand houndwork completely in order to hunt successfully, but learning as much as you can about it will greatly increase your pleasure.

prevent a nasty accident.

Do not fail to thank the M. F. H. at the end of the hunt for the day of sport. Most people also make a point of thanking the huntsman, and anyone else who has helped them out in the course of the day.

It isn't necessary to understand houndwork completely in order to hunt successfully and have a wonderful time doing it. Such an understanding will greatly increase your pleasure, and if you plan to hunt regularly it would be rather silly not to learn all you can about it. You can learn the terms and written explanation of procedures from books. However, you will learn most by keeping your eyes and ears open while you are actually hunting. ∎

CHAPTER THREE

GETTING YOURSELF AND YOUR HORSE TURNED OUT FOR THE HUNTER SHOW

Let's assume that you have a horse at a level to begin showing in some simple hunter classes, and that you ride well enough. First we must turn our attention to the matter of the physical preparations which you will need to make for yourself and your horse. Showing is one game in which a workmanlike appearance plays an important role. The immaculate, well-turned out horse and rider combination enters the ring with a tremendous advantage over less well-put-together competitors. So plan to acquire at least one good outfit. If your budget is too limited for this, probably you would do better to postpone your appearance in the show ring. The hunt attire described in the past chapter would get you by, if this is what you already have. However, you might look a bit overdressed for a medium-sized daytime horseshow. If you have a choice, a snappy-looking tweed jacket, brick or brown breeches, brown boots (the field boot variety are very popular now, and they do permit a lovely fit) form a good basic wardrobe for hunter shows. Boys and men look very nice in a plain tailored shirt and tie; in fact, the girls are copying them on this score at the moment. For girls and ladies, a ratcatcher (neckband) shirt is generally worn with a choker. If you can splurge a bit, have your choker monogrammed with your initials. Otherwise use a simple type of horsey pin to hold it in position, and avoid all other jewelry. No matter how small they are, take the earrings out of your pierced ears in the morning as you get ready for the show. Girls and ladies wear hairnets unless the hair is very short, or in braids, or tucked up inside the hat. You will need a velvet hard hat and could choose black, brown, or navy blue to complement your jacket. Get along without chewing gum, even if it kills you, while you are in the show ring; there are few things that detract as much from an attractive appearance!

So much for you. How about your horse? As far as being clean, polished and trimmed, the same advice that you read in the chapter on hunting holds good. But while you may have a little less gear in one way, in others you will have a great deal more. You will want to take along grooming equipment, rub rags, and hoof dressing. You will need to carry hay and grain for feeding and buckets for water. Many people take their

A rider correctly turned out for a daytime hunter show.

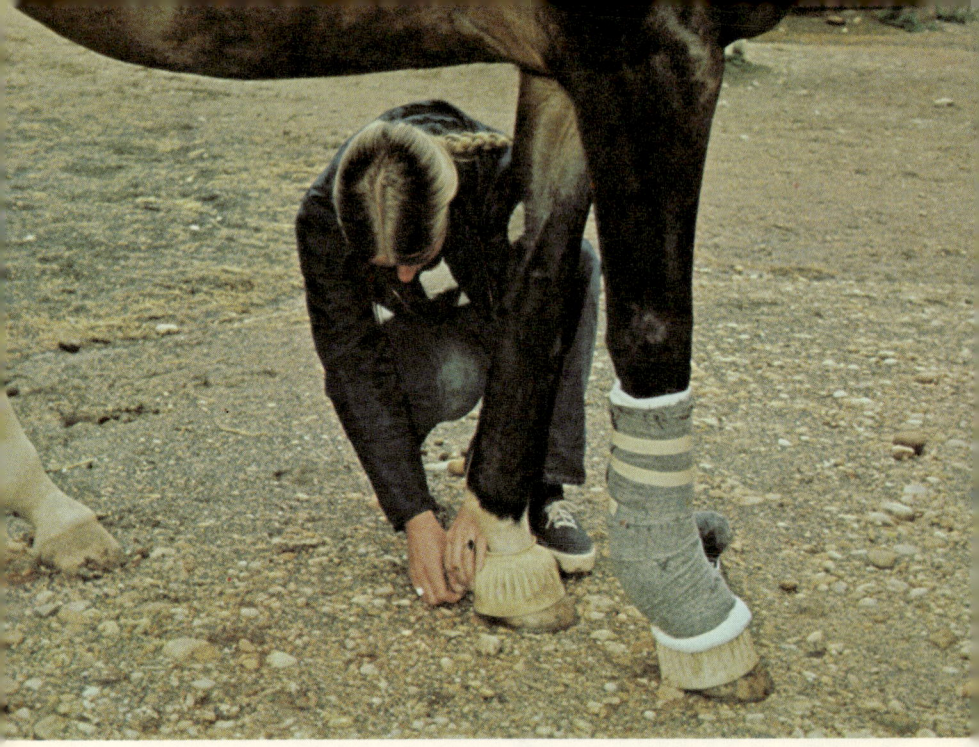

It is the custom to bandage the horse's legs to protect him, in case he scrambles in the trailer or van. Note the use of bell boots as an added precaution.

own water supply with them, as frequently the water at the show does not suit your horse. Obviously, if you are trailering or vanning, you will ship your horse in a halter and carry along his tack. Don't forget to have a lead shank on hand. It is the custom to bandage the horse's legs to protect him, in case he scrambles in the trailer or van. There are many types of bandages, but probably the knit track bandages are the most usual, put on carefully from the coronary band to the knee and padded with "cottons" or some other type of concussion-absorbing material.

Now, contrary to the custom of saving "the best for last" we have saved the "worst for last" (or at least the most complicated part) in describing your preparations for showing in the hunter division. This is the convention of braiding. The unfortunate part of the whole situation is that if other horses are braided, yours will look positively scroungy if you do not braid. And this does take practice. However, it is not beyond the capabilities even of twelve-year-old children. There is at least one well-known summer riding camp where the children must braid a horse or pony every day until the appearance is "professional." This means that they must practice until they can "do up" a horse or pony well enough to appear at a show, looking well turned out. It develops that these young people have the assignment licked in less than one week. So, take heart! With just a little concentrated effort you too will be able to braid your horse so that no one can look down his—or her—nose at you.

Should you find yourself totally on your own, study the photographs of a well-braided mane and tail. Then remember a few basic things. Braiding is simply a matter of a number of tight little "pigtails" or plaits lying evenly on the off side of the horse's neck!

Here are some tips that might help you. Gather all your supplies before you begin. You'll need braiding needles—at least two. These can be purchased in any notions department if there is no tack shop nearby. Use tapestry needles with blunt ends, and heavy-duty thread—the 2 oz. size. Try to get the thread nearest to the color of your horse's mane. You'll also need to have a mane comb on hand, as well as an old hair brush for brushing the tail and getting all the hairs separated before starting. A long "clippie" (the type of hair clip that is used in beauty parlors) to hold back the mane you aren't working on at the moment makes it much easier as you do each braid. You will find dampening the mane helps too, so a small sponge is a good item to put in your braiding kit. Oh, yes, include a pair of scissors for snipping the thread (but never, never the mane). Another very handy item to have is a seam ripper for the time after the show when you have to undo your handiwork.

Incidentally, unless the mane has been recently pulled, you will have to do a bit in this direction before you commence your plaiting operation. Take a thin lock of hair, wrap it around your comb and pull it out. Repeat with the longest pieces until the entire mane is about five or six inches long. This process also thins the mane, which makes braiding easier.

So here you are ready to start. Brush the mane until it is as smooth as possible. Thread both needles (just for convenience) with about twelve inches of thread; then, with your mane comb, separate about an inch of mane, holding the rest back with a "clippie." Braid each little section of hair carefully and tightly, pulling it downwards all the time so that it will lie flat when it is finished. When you reach the bottom of the braid, take your needle and sew through it, winding the thread around the little ends a few times. Then fold them back, under the braid, wind around them again, and sew through the whole business once more. Next, double the braid under, bring your needle up from under the base of the braid and take one or two stitches first from one side, then the other. Now you can tie off the thread and snip it, although if you want to be absolutely sure that the braid will stay in exact position, take a stitch or two in the middle. (By the way, as you braid be sure to hold your hands as close to the horse's neck as possible and to plait *straight* down.) If the completed braid is about the size of a cigarette and has no bristly little tufts of hair protruding and is flat on the horse's neck, you've done an excellent job.

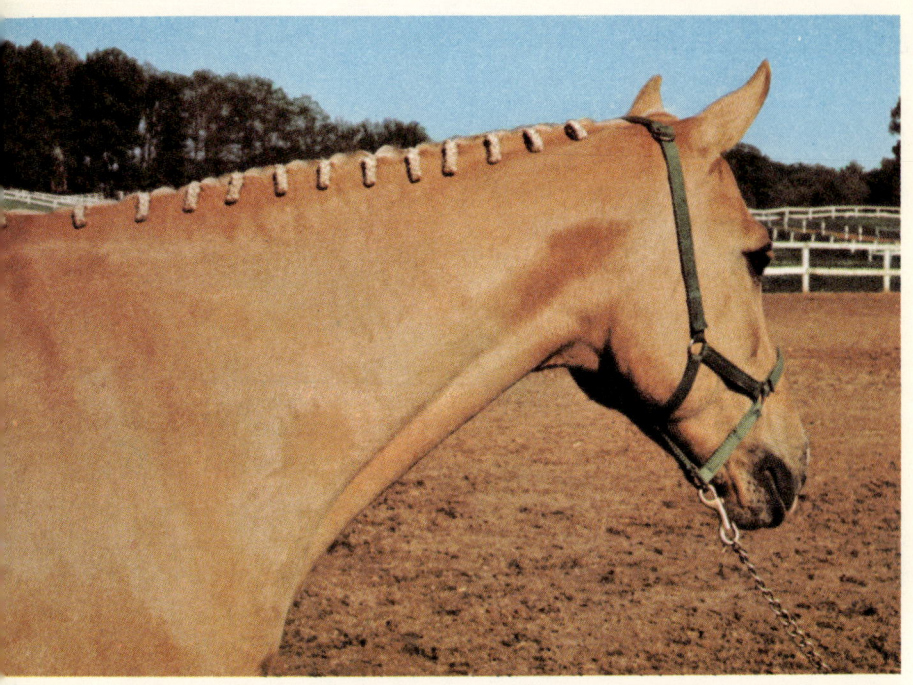

If the completed braid is about the size of a cigarette, and lies flat on the neck with no bristly little tufts of hair protruding, you've done an excellent job.

If not, use that handy little seam ripper and start all over again, braiding more tightly, pulling down harder and tying the thread tighter still. It may seem hard at first, but when you and your horse jog into the ring to collect that ribbon, looking ever so elegant, with each little braid neat and even, you'll forget the cold, aching fingers and frustrating hours of rebraiding in the pleasure of having the ribbon pinned on your horse's beautiful head.

    Braiding the tail is more difficult to describe in writing. If you already know how to "French braid," you will find it greatly simplifies what looks like a very complicated procedure; however, you will still want to have professional help the first time or two. If you just can't master French braiding on your own and can't find someone to braid that tail for you, you will be all right entering the smaller shows with a well-washed tail that has been scrupulously brushed out until not one speck of straw or dust remains. Meanwhile, practice, practice, practice and practice some more is the order of the day, so that when, at long last, you are finally ready for a really big show, you will be able to whip out

If you already know how to "French braid," you will find it greatly simplifies what looks like a very complicated procedure. Best advise is: practice, practice, practice!

a lovely braided tail in ten minutes, wrap it with a damp tail bandage until time for your first class, and Voila! There you are, in the ring, elegantly turned out from the top of your head to the tip of your horse's tail.

At the end of the day of showing, you are not ready to settle down to your hot tub or other pleasures until the "last rites" have been performed for your horse. Unless you have a groom to take over, you will unload, unbandage and take down those twenty-two or so tiny braids so lovingly sewn in at about six o'clock that morning. A bracing rubdown for his legs is good (for *him,* that is!) if he has had a strenuous day of showing. You will feed him, and be sure that he is comfortably bedded. Now, at last you can turn towards the house and human comforts, and the inevitable rehash of the day.

So there it is—the business of getting yourself and your horse ready for, and back from, the horse show. Perhaps we have made it sound too formidable. As you drag your aching bones into bed, perhaps sixteen hours after you commenced your day, you might be telling yourself, "I'm nuts! It's all too much work." Right, right, sure it is—until the next weekend! ■

CHAPTER FOUR

WIN YOUR "UNDER SADDLE" CLASS!

If you are inexperienced in showing in any of the many hunter divisions, or if your horse is "green," you will probably want to start "on the flat" before you attempt to go over fences. Your best bet will be to seek out some unrecognized shows that will not affect your horse's or your status the subsequent year. These unrecognized shows are a sort of backyard practice ground and provide an excellent means of giving either rider or horse necessary experience before launching into serious competition.

What should your horse understand and be able to do before you try him even on the flat at a horse show? The requirements for the class sound very simple, but perhaps it is this very simplicity that makes *winning* difficult. The class specifications may read something like this: "Horses to be shown at a walk, trot and canter both ways of the ring. At least eight horses, if available, but never more than eight at one time, are required to gallop collectively one way of the ring. Martingales are not permitted. To be judged on performance, including manners and way of moving, and soundness." Sometimes it will also state that "horses are to be shown on light contact throughout" or it might read "contact with the horse's mouth is recommended throughout." Even if the specifications do not state this, contact has become an accepted procedure in hunter under saddle classes. The class description *may* also read "may be called on to back."

There will be one exception to the above description, which you can count on as a general rule. *Green* horses are not asked to gallop.

Now suppose we consider each of the requirements of the under saddle class, for, as we mentioned, winning the class will involve many factors, and may be very tough!

The horse must walk. Easy, isn't it? But he must look more impressive at a walk than any other animal in the ring. So the horse should be encouraged to walk out with long, ground-covering strides. If the rider overplays his hand, and urges the horse on too much, he may commence to gig or break into a trot; if the judge happens to see this, there goes that class! At a trot, the horse should look as if he is going somewhere and means to get there, so he should not "dog along." At the same time he should look relaxed and pleasant, even though reasonably energetic. If he zips along at such a fast trot that he is passing everything else in the

These horses are being "prepped" or "schooled" for *under saddle* class.

ring, once again, his goose is cooked! After walking and trotting, he will be asked to canter. Here there are even more rigid conventions. He *must* pick up an inside lead, or he is almost automatically out of the ribbons. (It will look as if his two legs toward the center of the ring are moving forward in advance of the other two. This is not the whole truth, but we can leave it at that until we go into the matter of how, precisely, the horse's legs do function at each gait.) At a canter, again, the horse should look businesslike and yet pleasant and agreeable; he should not be tearing along, nor on the other hand, loafing. When the command to walk is heard once more over the loudspeaker, he should come back to a walk promptly, and pleasantly. His mouth should stay closed and his head should retain a natural attitude.

Incidentally, the old custom was, invariably, to give the command "canter" from a walk, but this is no longer the rule. At least once during the course of the class the command to canter will be given while horses are walking, but more and more judges also give the command to canter from the trot. Actually, unless you have practiced this exercise carefully, not permitting the horse to increase the speed of the trot in preparation for the canter, the "wrong lead" is quite apt to occur.

Next, you may be asked to "hand gallop." A hand gallop is just a faster canter, and the term "hand gallop" probably originated to indicate that your horse is still very much "in hand" or under complete control. Some judges excuse a part of the class from the ring at this point. Normally, a group of eight animals—frequently the ones that have impressed the judge the most thus far—are called out first to "take the rail." After they are all situated and walking, the judge will say "canter." Very shortly thereafter, the command "Hand gallop, please!" will be heard. This is where many horses or ponies "blow up" and lose the class. Next the command "Halt, please!" rings out, and your horse should do precisely that, with no fussing around or shooting his nose up to the sky! If you are standing on the rail, you will notice that this is where the judge's eyes swivel around to try to see which animals stop promptly and in a mannerly fashion. Many times the decision between two places will be decided at this moment.

In the current requirements of the "under saddle" class, there is no mention made of backing the horse. However, this is asked for at many shows, so it is a good idea to be sure that your mount will back readily and pleasantly. (If he backs well, he will move straight back, head and neck in an essentially natural attitude, legs moving in diagonal pairs.)

The class description stated that it was to be "ridden on light contact." Since this small book is not designed as a course of instruction in riding and schooling, we simply have to assume that the rider is able to ride on contact. But perhaps one point should be emphasized. Riding on contact is not primarily a matter of a *tight rein*. It is most of all sufficient sensitivity in the hands to enable the rider to maintain just the lightest "feel" on the reins that are attached to the bit lying on the bars of the horse's mouth. Contact should not *restrict* movement; it should better the quality of the horse's movement, and at the same time communicate to the horse exactly what is desired in the way of increasing and decreasing speed and energy.

In addition to these technical requirements, there are innumerable other factors that will determine the four winning places. You have a tremendous advantage to begin with if your horse is a good mover. This, remember, means that he will seem to "slip along" with very little knee or hock action, and to strike the ground lightly, covering a lot of territory with long, low strides. Unfortunately, there is not too much that you can do about it if your horse really is not a good mover. You can, however, get him to move to the very best of his ability.

An attractive angle of head and neck is equally important. In the case of hunters, this means that he will travel with his head and neck somewhat extended as opposed to the extreme arch found in the Arabian or in the Saddle Horse. Most assuredly, you do not want him to travel with his nose pointing towards the sky or, almost as bad, his chin in against his chest. In most cases, both of these faults are the direct result of bad riding.

Besides the specifics described, there are a number of semi-intangibles or matters of strategy to be considered. You should ride into the ring with the attitude that you have the best schooled, best moving and best

A big smile accompanies third place honors, earned in very tough competition.

functioning mount there. Your whole attitude should indicate this. Businesslike, absorbed in your job, convinced that the judge will note all this —these are some of the psychic factors that enter into winning. Try to come in the gate alone, out of the bunch, and behave as if you are totally absorbed in going about your business—that of demonstrating the impressive performance of your mount. You must also indicate that it is obvious that you have a winner. While it is annoying to judges to have riders crowd around them (and for this reason, if no other, you should hug the rail most of the time) at some point in a large class when your mount is working at his very best, it may become necessary to take an inside track. There may be thirty or forty animals in the ring, and the judge or judges *must* get a look at yours if you hope to win.

Remember, as much as possible, try to stay off by yourself while you are in the ring. It's terribly awkward to find yourself boxed in when the command "Canter, please" is heard! Then too, many horses object to being crowded, and having your horse kick at another is not exactly the way to create a good impression. If you are having any small problems, minimize them. Don't make faces that give away your discomfiture. If your horse makes a mistake, correct it as quickly and as unobtrusively as possible. If he tends to be a bit rapid at a canter, go extra deep into

Horse and rider nicely turned out for either a hunter horsemanship, or performance class over fences. For an under saddle class, or horsemanship on the flat, the rider would remove the martingale.

your corners so that you do not seem to be whizzing past everyone else. Sometimes an unobtrusive circle or two (always maintaining gait) is a good device if your horse is too speedy. Remember, too, that you can always cut across the ring and relocate yourself in an empty spot on the rail if you are in a very congested clump of horses.

Don't forget that one very important factor is your horse's manners. While kicking at another is a very obvious breach of good manners, there are many other less tangible aspects. Soft, pleasant halting or slowing down is part of good manners in the horse. And unfair as it seems, a horse traveling with the ears pinned back, giving a sour impression, sometimes is knocked out of the ribbons for this reason alone. It is almost impossible to tell anyone just how to induce his horse to be cheerful about his work but you can make every effort not to do things that are bound to irritate him. Just to mention a few, "snapping him in the mouth" with every stride because your hands do not follow the movements of his head, or swinging on his mouth, or gouging him accidentally with spurs or clutching his sides with your heels—any and all of these things will predispose him to look sulky. ∎

CHAPTER FIVE

WHAT HAPPENS AT A WALK, TROT AND CANTER AND AT THEIR VARIATIONS ?

In the previous chapter, we mentioned that your horse would be asked to walk, trot, canter, and to hand gallop. What is happening in each case? Furthermore, you have probably heard of "gaited" horses and that hunters are not gaited horses. But then you have heard the expression that a certain hunter has excellent gaits, or that he should be kept under control at all gaits. So perhaps all this needs a bit of clarification.

The horse's "natural gaits" are considered the walk, trot and gallop. While it is often spoken of as walk, trot and canter (a slower gallop), "cantering," when maintained for fairly long periods, is mostly developed in the horse by humans. The animal who performs only at these gaits, contradictory as it may seem, is not considered a gaited horse. (Thoroughbreds, for example, are not considered "gaited.") Horses are termed "gaited horses" when they have been taught by humans to adapt these standard ways of moving by certain changes or additions to them. One thinks most of all of the five-gaited American Saddle Horse as the real "gaited" horse. To the walk, trot and canter have been added two other ways of moving the legs. These additional gaits are most commonly called "slow gait" and "rack." In our consideration of hunters, these particular patterns of leg movements need not concern us.

It is not only nice but very useful to know exactly how your horse's legs are moving under him—and under you. It is perfectly possible to ride all your life and not understand precisely what is happening; however, when and if you get into the matter of schooling your horse in an effort to produce better movement, this knowledge becomes almost essential.

Aside from that, animal movement—particularly that animal that we are considering—is a fascinating topic in its own right. If, on the other hand, this subject does not particularly interest you, you can simply "skim" this chapter, learning enough to understand when your horse is on what is commonly termed the correct lead, and to understand when he has become disunited, or has performed a "flying change" of leads, or if he is maintaining a counter gallop.

We will begin with the slowest of the three gaits—the walk. Perhaps the simplest way to describe what is happening is to say that the horse

Horse moving at a relaxed walk. You are seeing the tri-pedal support phase — to be followed by the bi-pedal support. The left hind will lift, then the right fore will ground.

will push off with one hind leg (his "motor" or "drive" is in the hind end) followed by the foreleg on that side, followed by the hind leg on the other side, followed by the foreleg on *that* side and so on and on as long as he is walking. You can start "counting off" anywhere you wish. Assuming that you start with the left hind, the sequence will be as follows: left hind, left front, right hind and right front, etc. We consider this a four beat gait; it is quite smooth, and the rider need only sit, perhaps squeezing with alternate legs to improve the energy of his horse's stride, and permitting his hands to follow the balancing gestures of the horse's head and neck.

The pattern of leg movements of the trot is the easiest (and perhaps the only) gait that you can actually catch with the naked eye. At this gait, the horse's diagonally opposite legs move forward and strike the ground simultaneously, in a way that results in two beats only and a period of suspension. The speed of the ordinary trot is between that of the walk and the gallop. But we humans have also taught our horses to maintain this gait at a slower speed and again at a faster speed. So we speak of three speeds of a trot. In hunter seat horsemanship classes, the rider may be asked to demonstrate these three speeds. They are termed slow or "collected" (usually ridden as a "sitting trot"), ordinary (usually ridden as a posting trot), and a third speed in which the rider encourages his horse

This is a good trot! The diagonal pairs are striking the ground in unison.

to extend the stride without permitting him to escape into a canter. Consequently, he does cover more ground in a given length of time, and while this does result in more speed, (i.e., he moves from point A to point B in less time as a result of fewer strides than he would at an ordinary trot) the speed is the end result, not the requirement of the movement. The legs should not be moving faster but with a longer swing. The essence of the movement lies in these lengthened strides, with no loss of quality. In the horsemanship class, the judge will probably use the term extended; or he might use the word "strong" instead. Unless he specifically states whether it is to be ridden posting or sitting, the rider may elect whichever he finds more effective.

There are several other terms used to designate the various ways in which a horse may be asked to trot. For example, in western classes, you will hear of a "jog" trot; in dressage competitions, you will also hear of a "working trot." Translated into the hunt seat equitation rider's language, the jog trot would be a rather slow, short striding trot to which the rider would normally sit; the working trot is just a slightly slow variation of the ordinary trot.

The individual who is showing a hunter under saddle need be concerned with one speed of the trot only—the ordinary. The contestant in hunter seat horsemanship classes almost certainly will—if asked to demonstrate three speeds of a trot—hear them called collected (or slow), ordinary and extended.

And now let's take a close look at that third gait—the canter. The canter has almost, but not exactly, the same mechanics as the gallop. It

35

is the gait that you need to understand the most thoroughly, so we will consider it before we discuss the gallop. You could start "counting off" at any of several points, but it is simplest to start mentally with a hind foot. A slow motion camera will show you the following sequence of events: assuming that you start watching as the right hind moves under the horse, for a fraction of a second it will be the only leg on the ground. It will be followed by what is termed the right diagonal pair (in considering diagonals, one counts off from the *front* leg, so this means the right front and left hind) striking the ground at the same time—so now our horse is on three legs for a split instant, before he lifts the original leg to have struck the ground (the right hind) leaving him on a diagonal pair only. Obviously this can't last long, so now he throws forward his one remaining leg to catch his balance and continue the forward movement —his left front. So once again he is on three legs before he lifts the diagonal pair and lastly is supported by that one leg only—the left foreleg. Immediately following this, there will be a split second interval when all four legs are in the air, known as the period of suspension, before the same pattern commences again.

The process that we have just described is known as "cantering on the left lead" and is the lead required in under saddle classes when the horse is on the track to the left. By track to the left, just remember that your left hand, leg, etc., will be towards the center of the ring. Standing in the middle of the ring, it will look as if the horse's two inside legs (left in this case) are moving forward ahead of his outside legs. Eventually, you should be able to feel this when you are mounted, even without sneaking a downward glance.

You will hear the expression that a horse is "leading with his right (or left) foreleg." Actually, this leg is the *last* leg to move up and support him in order to complete the stride. However, we should point out that many times before that hind leg commences the one, two, three beats of the canter, the horse may take a preparatory step with the front leg that will be the *final* leg to support his weight before the instant of suspension. In any event, the expression "leading with the right (or left) leg" is such a commonly accepted term that we will use it in this sense.

When you take the track to the right, and require a right lead, the entire process described will be reversed. The horse will commence with his left hind, followed by the left diagonal pair and lastly will strike the ground with his right front.

If you study newspaper pictures of race horses on the track, you will be able to find every phase that we have just described. And while all of this may sound complicated to a human, luckily it doesn't seem that way to the horse. Even little foals anywhere from a few hours to a few days old will have this all figured out and will be found galloping along beside

The canter at instant of suspension. Changing from a trot to a canter is an exercise which must be practiced in order to avoid taking the wrong lead.

their mothers in the field. In order to thoroughly understand this and to make use of it in your riding, you will need to trace it out mentally many times before it becomes really clear to you.

Obviously, there should be a reason that a horse is expected to canter on a right lead when on the track to the right and a left when on the track to the left, in his hack classes. The reason becomes more apparent when you watch the horse at a gallop.

The only way in which the actual pattern will vary at a gallop from that of a canter is in the behavior of the diagonal pair of legs. Instead of striking the ground simultaneously, the hind leg will ground a fraction of a second ahead of its diagonally opposite member. Thus at a gallop you will have four beats instead of the three that we described at a canter. At a gallop, when the horse is moving faster, on bends, it will be fairly simple to see that he is leaning a little towards the inside of the turn. It will be easier for him to keep his balance as he has what looks like, and is called, a leading leg toward the inside—the direction in which he is leaning slightly. This "leading leg" actually supports the entire weight of the body for a split second; the horse uses it as a pole vaulter might use a pole, (not an original figure of speech on my part, incidentally),* to carry him into the air for that instant of suspension. The weight

---

* See *"Training Hunters, Jumpers and Hacks"* by Brig. Gen. Harry D. Chamberlin. Chapter 1, section entitled *"The Gallop."*

is heavier on that side, and he needs to bring that last leg out there as a sort of prop. It is really the same principle that we find in skiing, skating or even running as we make turns. While at the slower speed of a canter it is not an urgent necessity, most horses are more comfortable on what we term an inside lead, and convention has it that in hunter classes under saddle, he *must* be on this lead.

Your hunter seat horsemanship class will be a different story. Here you may be asked to pick up an inside lead, interrupt and follow with an outside lead, and interrupt again with another change of leads. It is entirely possible that this will put your horse on an outside lead around a bend. He should hold this lead, when called for. Such a way of moving is properly termed the counter gallop (or counter canter) and may also correctly be called the false gallop (or false canter). It is *not* a disunited gallop or canter since the legs follow the correct sequence of a canter or gallop. Nor is it properly termed a "wrong lead" when it is the lead that was asked for. It would be a "wrong lead" in an under saddle class, because it would not be the lead demanded. The well-schooled horse should take whichever lead is asked for by his rider, regardless of the location of the rail, or if he is in the middle of the ring where there is no rail! In spite of this fact, because in hack or under saddle classes, he will be asked for inside leads only, the outside lead (counter gallop) is commonly referred to simply as "the wrong lead."

There is a third, very uncomfortable and awkward way for the horse to canter or gallop, and this is referred to as a DISUNITED canter (or gallop) or as a "CROSS CANTER." It occurs if the horse is not sufficiently agile for a flying change of leads with a change of directions, and is not permitted to come to a trot and recommence on an inside lead. Since there is often confusion as to what actually happens in such situations, flying change and disunited canter deserve special consideration.

What is a "flying change?" In a true flying change, the rearrangement of the pattern in which the legs will follow one another must, of necessity, be accomplished during that fleeting instant of suspension when no leg at all is on the ground. Otherwise, it is not really a "FLYING" change. Thinking of it in this way may help you to understand the process. For only when the horse is airborne and not already committed to a particular leg following a particular leg to maintain his balance— only then is he in a position to change the pattern from that of the last cantering stride and reverse the order in which his feet will strike the ground. Occasionally, you will notice that a horse changes in front and one or two strides later, does manage to rearrange his hind legs to coincide with what his front legs are doing. This is not a true flying change, but for practical purposes, within a stride or two, it will have accomplished the same purpose. What actually happened was a few disunited strides which he managed to correct—a somewhat difficult feat, incidentally.

Now let's follow exactly what happens in a correctly executed flying change. Suppose we have our horse cantering on the right lead. This would mean that if he were to continue on this lead, he would continue to move his left hind leg under his body followed by the left diagonal pair (left front and right hind) grounding simultaneously followed by his right front followed by the period of suspension and then he would recommence the same series of leg movements all over again. But suppose that he needs to switch to the left lead for the sake of more secure balance as he turns to the left. During that instant in the air between the time that the last forefoot struck the ground and was lifted and a hind leg once more moved under him, he must reverse what he was doing on the previous strides. So now he must bring his right hind leg under his body first (instead of the left), followed this time by the *right front and left hind* striking the ground together, to be followed, lastly, by the left foreleg. And here he is, all comfortably situated on the left lead!

The process that we have just described is the ideal way for a change of directions to be accomplished when the canter or gallop must be maintained without interruption. But there are other things that may, and all too frequently do, occur.

Many show ring hunters are not sufficiently agile to accomplish a flying change— little western horses frequently make our hunters look rather silly in this direction —and may switch the forelegs only, producing a disunited canter. We will need to trace what happens in this situation. First, we must consider once again a horse cantering along on a right lead and needing to make an abrupt turn to the left without breaking gait. If the horse lacks the ability, either through insufficient training or insufficient talent, to accomplish a flying change, the hind legs will probably continue in the same pattern of first striking the ground with the left hind (as he normally would for a right lead); but next, instead of grounding the *left diagonal pair* (left front, right hind), he strikes the ground with the *right lateral* pair (right front and right hind), since he is saving that left front to catch his balance as he turns to the left. It is as if he has not been able to plan ahead enough to rearrange his hind legs while he was "airborne"; he feels that he must catch his balance by throwing that left leg out last as he turns left. In his defense, we should recall that the full weight of his body will be sustained on that foreleg for a fraction of a second; to his "mind," this is the best that he can do at this precise moment. However, this means of locomotion feels positively ghastly to the rider, looks uncoordinated and must be uncomfortable for the horse; generally it will produce an awkward jump. Most assuredly, on a hunter round, this horse will not get a star for his "way

The pony has been circling right, on a right lead. Now, a turn to the left is being made, and (while in the air) he is rearranging the entire pattern to that for a left lead—a flying change shown at the instant of suspension.

of going."

So there is the story of the canter and gallop, the flying change and the disunited canter or gallop. To school a horse well, it is important that the rider should be able to *feel* all of this happening under him as well as to grasp it mentally. To thoroughly understand the more complicated gaits (canter and gallop) and their variations, one will need to make a concentrated study of this chapter. Try to visualize your horse in a familiar location and then follow the sequence of movements, a leg at a time.

For a quick review, we will summarize. At a walk (a four beat gait), assuming that you start counting with the right hind, the rhythm will be: right hind, right front, left hind, left front and so on.

At a trot, you have two beats only and a period of suspension; diagonal pairs will be raised and strike the ground simultaneously. When the diagonal pairs do not ground at precisely the same instant, you have a trot of poor quality. This is usually called a disconnected trot.

At a canter you have three beats. Assuming that you start counting with the right hind leg, the rhythm will be: right hind, right diagonal pair (right front and left hind) striking the ground simultaneously, and lastly the left foreleg, followed by a period of suspension. This produces the left lead.

A gallop—the same as a canter except that the hind foot of the diagonal pair grounds a split second ahead of its diagonally opposite member. This produces a four beat gait.

Occasionally a canter takes the same form. The horse's legs, even though the *speed* of a canter is maintained, may function as in a gallop. That is to say, the hind leg may ground a fraction of a second ahead of its diagonally opposite member during the second beat. This produces a four beat canter and a very uncomfortable situation for the rider. It is termed a *disconnected* (but not disunited) canter. The fact that the horse's legs normally do function with these four beats at a gallop is one of several reasons that the rider generally stays somewhat up off the horse's back at this speed. An extreme example of this is the position of the jockey.

A flying change is correctly executed at a canter and gallop during the period of suspension, by *reversing* the left and right order in which the hind legs will strike the ground and consequently reversing the rest of the cantering pattern. One reads that the horse must "change with the front and the hind legs at the same time." This simply means that the horse should change the entire pattern during the fleeting instant of suspension, when he is in the air.

A disunited (cross) canter is generally produced by the horse switching the order in which the front legs strike the ground without making the appropriate change with the hind legs. (Occasionally a disunited canter occurs in slowing down when the horse drops too much weight on the forehand and switches the order in which the hind legs are moving under him.) When this happens, a lateral, instead of a diagonal pair moves forward at the same time. In a disunited canter the sequence would be, for example: left hind, *right lateral* pair and finally the left front. This is an awkward and uncomfortable way of moving for horse and rider.

A counter canter (or counter gallop) is also properly termed a false canter (or false gallop). This indicates that the horse is leading with an outside as opposed to an inside leg along the arc of a circle. It is properly termed a "wrong lead" at any time that the rider has asked for an inside lead; this is most conspicuously the case in under saddle or hack classes. ■

CHAPTER SIX

"BIG TIME" HUNTER AND JUMPER COURSES

Let's take a look at some typical "big time" hunter and jumper courses, and consider some of the requirements of riding them. This type of competition most definitely is not for the neophyte in the saddle. None the less, it is all to the good to be as widely informed as possible, in order to follow the show as a spectator and in anticipation of the day in which you will be a participant.

First, let's discuss the technical differences between those courses termed "hunter" as opposed to "jumper." In theory, obstacles on hunter courses are designed to simulate those found in actual foxhunting. While the colorful "hunter" courses found at a large show may not bear much similarity to the country and fences over which horses really hunt, still there are some very definite conventions governing the type of obstacles which may be used. Those most likely to be encountered include chicken coops, rustic rails, brush jumps, gates of all descriptions, sheep hurdles, aikens, pens, simulated stone walls, banks, ditches—in fact, man-made replicas of just about anything and everything that one might encounter in riding cross country. The in-and-out type of combination will be found on virtually every well-planned hunter course. This combination is generally composed of brown rustic fences, and the original idea was that these two fences approximated the old country lane that one might cross in hunting. The theory is that a hunter should be able to jump himself out of any spot that he jumped himself into. Now, however, our horse show courses have reached a stage of admitted artificiality. The current A. H. S. A. rule permits the rider, in a situation where his horse has refused the second element, the choice of having the horse jump himself out of an in-and-out or going around the first element and trying the two as a unit once again.

Since the big horse show is designed to be a spectator attraction, every effort is made to have the courses as colorful and dramatic as possible. This is half of the fun. It should be immaterial to the well-schooled show ring hunter whether the little garden gate is flanked with brilliant pots of flowers, or if it is presented in more drab outline. The "big show" participant must be prepared for sights (moving spot lights, flash bulbs, fluttering decorations) and sounds (throngs of spectators, music, applause) that would shatter the nerves of a less sophisticated show goer!

Rail fence jump made to look as "natural" as possible on this outside hunter course.

Now, let's take a look at some jumper courses. Generally the course itself will be more intricate, plus the fact that you will see an even wider range of yet more colorful obstacles. And the type of fences will be quite different. Striped poles, perhaps placed on two sets of standards, and parallel to one another, may very nearly create an optical illusion. A wildly painted, sloping panel may be followed by a straight vertical fence. There may be a very architectural gate set between massive (simulated) brick gateposts, followed by a sharp turn and a triple in-and-out; hogs backs, double oxers, triple bars—all may be part of the courses.

The modern jumper course is designed to require a great deal more than just the ability to jump a big fence. It is designed to require a very high level of schooling in quick maneuverability. The horse must be able to "come back" where necessary and to "pick up impulse" in the matter of one stride. It also requires the ability to gallop and jump at speed in the "jump off" under certain sets of rules. Fences found on good jumper courses of today require of the horse both the ability to get up over a big fence and the scope to jump a wide spread. Modern jumper courses are designed to pose real problems of strategy for the rider, similar to a problem of mathematics. How many strides should he go for between fence seven and eight? If he "brings his horse in close" for the take-off for the triple, can he gallop along and meet the vertical fence right, in three strides? Or should he check on landing, and ride for four strides? When he is riding against time in a jump-off, how short can he turn between fence five and six to be sure that no one turns inside his path, and beats his time by a fraction of a second? Competing in the "big time"

It is important to school your hunter over as many different types of obstacles as possible.

jumper classes becomes a highly specialized game, requiring the rider to keep a cool head for planning and executing, a terrific eye for distance and a sharp sense of timing. In addition, he must have the courage to make the daring move when and where it becomes necessary. Actually, the same *qualities* are important in the first-rate rider in hunter classes; however, the math required is much simpler. Naturally, from the spectator's point of view, the jumper classes are far more exciting. There is more color, more drama, frequently more speed, and in general, there may be more "spills and thrills."

However, the successful rider in hunter competitions has a few problems that do not concern the jumper rider. In the hunter class, the rider must make the horse look good. He must manage to adjust the speed throughout to get as even a pace as possible, and at the same time, he must manage to have his mount arrive at every fence standing off just enough to have the arc of the fence come out exactly right. That is, the arc of the jump made by the horse should reach its apex at the top of the fence; the horse should leave the ground as far from the fence on the take-off side as he lands on the other side; the overall trajectory of an ideal hunter jump should give the impression of a smooth semicircular loop. He will be penalized if the jump is too long and flat and again if the

Working hunter on the outside course. Note how economically he jumps, with forelegs tightly folded.

horse noticeably shortens the last stride and takes off so close to the fence that it becomes squarish. In addition, the style in which the horse handles his body over the fence is important. His front legs should be folded together neatly at the top of the fence. Dangling legs, or legs that seem to scramble, incur a heavy penalty. The head and neck, in general, should be extended, as opposed to jumping with the head in the air, which generally produces a caved-in back and poor folding of front legs.

Besides all of this, the horse should look as if he gallops and jumps effortlessly, and must create an impression of being comfortable to ride over fences. Ideally, it should look as if he just happens to arrive at a good line of take-off for every fence; he should move along as if he has his mind on his job and means to get where he is going, neither tearing nor loafing along. He should look as if he is pleasant and safe to ride (the old expression was "an agreeable mount to hounds"), with a comfortable way of going—not pounding the ground or moving with high knee action—but galloping with long, low, easy strides. You hear the expression that a horse has "a lovely way of just slipping over the ground." The horse should also give the impression of being under control at all times, so that he could be halted between fences if required to do so.

So, as you see, the rider in competitive hunter classes has a few things to think about, too! Perhaps I should add that we will rarely see the ideal that has been described! ■

CHAPTER SEVEN

RIDING A SIMPLE HUNTER COURSE

We have discussed the type of courses in a general sense that one might find at a big show. Much of the trappings are purely theater, and the small outdoor horse show in which you compete may actually hold many of the same distances and problems as the big show. The courses will look less impressive and frequently are not as well planned and carefully laid out. Sometimes flimsy hunter fences will be used that are an invitation to a horse to jump carelessly.

One similarity that you will notice in hunter courses at both small unrecognized shows and big indoor ones is the fact that the hunter fences are flanked by wings, while the jumper fences are not. This convention is derived from the fact that normally in field hunting the horse will not be asked to take a narrow obstacle set out in the middle of a field all by itself. In actual hunting, what the horse must negotiate is more likely to be set into a fence line, or perhaps to be a section of a fallen tree. The hunter course, you will remember, presumably is testing the hunter over the *type* of obstacles that he might encounter out hunting.

The casual use of one other term may have confused you. "Fences" are by no means literally fences, but this too is simply horse show parlance. "Fences" used in this sense refers to anything that the horse may be required to jump in the show ring. The horizontal bars, the triple, etc., would be referred to as the sixth and eighth *fences,* for example, as well as the plain rustic or the gate that you will find on the hunter course.

Let us take a look at a typical hunter course of a sort that you might find, more or less dressed up depending on the occasion, at everything from the small, backyard show to the very large, fancy one. The competition will not be as keen at the small show, but basically, the factors involved in riding this course will be much the same wherever you may find a version of it—and this is practically anywhere.

The description of this particular class reads: "NOVICE HUNTERS in the ring. To be shown over eight fences at approximately 3'3". To be judged on performance and manners. Course B."

If we assume that your horse is capable of handling a course at the regulation height for its particular division, and assume, moreover, that you are capable of riding securely and nonabusively over it, the crux of the whole matter lies in getting the horse to the proper line of take-off with just sufficient energy to make a comfortable jump at every fence, and to move steadily between them. This is not nearly as simple as it sounds, because it requires an "eye" to estimate distance on the part of the rider and a horse that is schooled to a level where he not only jumps capably, but will lengthen and shorten strides in response to the rider's (ideally almost imperceptible) signals.

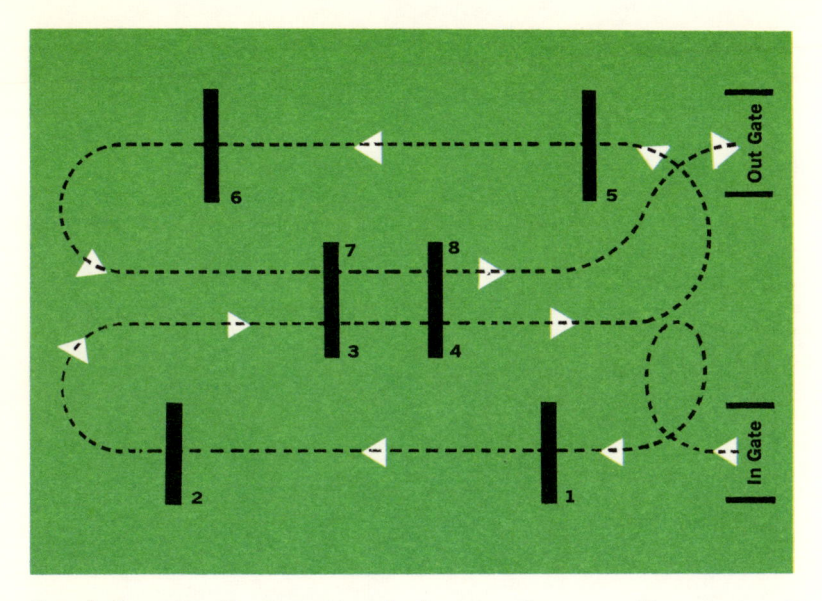

However, each individual must be realistic and recognize his own limitations as well as those of his horse. If you are inexperienced in showing hunters over fences, an effort on your part to "rate" the horse, bringing him to the proper line of take-off, will be beyond you and almost certainly will just mess up your horse. This is why, in the early stages of your showing, it is important to have a very well-schooled, safe jumping hunter, who will handle the problems of the course on his own. Your part will be to, first of all, study the chart (usually near the in-gate) carefully in order to have the course memorized totally—so totally that when you enter the ring you can follow the desired path without consciously thinking about it, even if you "blank out" a bit in the excitement of the moment. Secondly, watch a few rounds. You may note careless mistakes made by others—for example, slicing off the corners of the ring in such a way that a particular horse had a bad approach to a fence. While "rating" or "placing" will be beyond your ability for quite a while, staying on a particular path, without cutting corners, should not be. You might observe the effect of a badly planned entrance circle that got horse and rider off to a bad start. Having made all your mental notes go and warm up your horse immediately before entering the ring. Never stand frozen at the in-gate the last five minutes or so before your go—move around so that your horse is alert and functioning as you enter the ring and commence your circle. This does not imply that five minutes of warming up is all that is needed before commencing a round over fences. Some horses need quite a bit of work before a class; some are better off with a minimum, depending upon the temperament of the horse. There will be a considerable difference between the amount of work that the same horse needs before his first class of the day, and, let's say, his fourth. In the latter case, it is possible that the five minutes just before your entrance will be all that he needs for that particular class. In any event, you should enter the ring with your horse awake and his attention on his job. Now, as a "green" rider yourself, you need to fix *your* attention on following the path that you rode in your imagination, in sitting quietly, and simply keeping the horse moving at a comfortable rate of speed. You will try at all costs not to do anything that will make jumping a bad experience for him, such as snapping back and catching him in the mouth. You will be ready to make your move *with* him over the fence, avoiding getting too eager, hustling him or getting ahead of him. In other words you don't want to jump until he does. Again, you don't want to wait until you are left behind—this almost guarantees you a bad jump, if not a refusal, at the next fence.

Suppose you do get a refusal—what is your best strategy? If your horse backs readily, it almost always seems to work to back four or five steps without turning the horse away from the fence at all; then squeeze, encourage and quickly go again. Don't fuss around and turn on a big circle, repeating the same approach; the horse, having refused once, finding himself in the same situation, is predisposed to behave in the same way—and to refuse again! Of course, there is no absolute rule. If the horse really is a very willing jumper and stopped in front of the fence only because the rider seemed uncertain and he was "in wrong," he will probably take the fence the next try whether you circle or back. If he stopped because he has suffered abuse at your hands, such as being snagged in the mouth repeatedly, he naturally will be much less eager to go on again, no matter what you do. By and large, the technique of backing seems the most effective method of correcting a refusal.

If you have gotten a refusal, you pretty surely are out of the ribbons in any case. The important thing is to try to figure out just why your horse stopped. Get a more experienced friend to watch you to help you to discover just what particular things you are doing that are inspiring the lack of confidence in your horse. Very few inexperienced riders are

Too many strides between fences can result in a "proppy" fence, i.e., taking off too close to the object being jumped.

able to analyze their own mistakes.

Now let's look at the course and its problems as a more "show wise" rider might consider it. Let's assume that you are that more experienced rider, and that you have put in your number to go fifth. You are riding a rather small "Novice" hunter; she stands about 15 hands 2 inches. By watching a few rounds before you ride the course, you may be able to find out various things that will help you when you enter. First you notice what sort of an entrance circle was made. How deep did the rider have to go into the corner to get a good approach to his first fence? Did the fact that he angled off the corner too much result in the "proppy" (close) fence, with a bad arc? As a result of this poor beginning, this horse will not be a good one for you to watch to count the cantering strides between fence one and two as you had planned to do. He landed too close on the far side of the brush jump. Added to this, he seems to waver as he proceeds from fence one to fence two. So he is really traveling a longer path than he needs, and therefore will have more strides in any case. Not a good horse to watch to help you decide how you will try to ride the course!

Next, you watch a nice big horse who seems to know exactly what he is doing from the minute he enters the gate. He starts a comfortably large circle, makes a good approach to his first fence, and is over in excellent style. He moves very steadily to his second fence and you count the strides (you get the impression of a series of loops, and can count them even by watching the rider's hard hat) and find that he arrived at a good take-off distance for the second fence after five strides. The first horse had had seven, but you knew that this was way too many as a result of his "wandering." As the big horse comes down to the in-and-out in the center, he is moving a bit strongly and makes another bold fence over the first element of the in-and-out. But the space allotted for the one stride between is not enough to suit this particular horse "moving on" as much as he is. For the second element he is too close, and so "chips out." That is to say, he is too nearly "under" the second fence to make a jump of good arc. His fences five and six come out well enough with five strides between, but once more his rider must make his way through the tight in-and-out. This time, the rider attempts to check his horse a bit as he rounds the last bend, in an effort to shorten the stride enough to get through this combination successfully. But his horse has been moving rather strongly throughout and now is heading home; he does not respond kindly to this effort. So, inevitably, once again the in-and-out is the real trap. This time, whether by good luck or good planning, it is difficult to determine, the horse "stood back" on his first fence enough so that he landed fairly close to the first, had one good stride between and managed the "out" fence reasonably well. While it was not desirable to stand back as much as he did on the first element, the combination looked smoother this time than the first time that he went through.

As for you on the rail, watching and waiting your own turn to go in, you have learned several things. This big horse with quite a long stride had five comfortable strides between the combinations along the rail but he found the in-and-out tight. So with your smaller horse whose stride is not as long, you can reasonably expect to have no particular problem with the distance of the in-and-out at your horse's comfortable speed, if you meet the first element right. But what about the stretch along the rail? You are sure that your horse cannot manage it in five, but will you arrive in five and a half, so that you get a dreadful "proppy" fence, if you let your horse move along at his usual speed? Here comes another horse that is approximately the same size as yours. Perhaps this will give you the answer. And it does precisely that. The third horse, that has about the same stride as your horse, did move right along and did arrive at the second fence on a short sixth stride that produced a short fence. So you have learned that you should stay a little slow and arrive at fences two and six in such a way that you have a comfortable take-off from your sixth stride. You may have to check slightly for one or two strides after landing over your first and your fifth fences to accomplish this.

This is the type of observation and simple math that makes riding

Capable hunter shown at the phase of the jump in which the legs begin to unfold.

even apparently "easy" courses both difficult and fascinating. And where you have rounded a bend, as you have each time that you approached your in-and-out, you have no way of counting from the fence before. Here, the rider does best to try to stay a little slow on the turn and begin to estimate by "eye" as he approaches the combination. This "eye," which is the ability to judge distances by sight, develops slowly in most riders.

With luck, the horse just might happen to arrive right at every fence —but he will have to be awfully lucky! Doing anything to insure this, and doing it so subtly that it is not obvious, is the real reason why certain riders are almost constantly in the winning circle. It is totally impossible until you are so secure and sure of yourself over a course of jumps that you are virtually never left behind and never get ahead of your horse. This sort of riding begins to happen when you are so experienced that the fence itself becomes almost incidental; it is the total planning and execution of the course that absorbs your attention. In the early stages, it was exciting just to get into the ring and compete over fences. At a different stage, when you become aware of the various factors that will go into a winning performance and can do something about them, riding courses becomes engrossing most of all as a matter of strategy. ■

CHAPTER EIGHT

KNOW THE RULES OF THE GAME YOU PLAY

The fantastic growth of horse shows—and particularly of horse shows that are predominantly hunter—has, as we pointed out earlier, resulted in a diversity of classes and conditions that can become positively bewildering to the newcomer to the show ring. Sometimes an innocent lack of understanding of the rules can create very embarrassing situations.

One of the most frequent causes of chagrin—and sometimes extreme unpleasantness—is a lack of understanding of the horse show interpretation of the words "green" and "novice" and of the restrictions they entail. According to the A. H. S. A. rule book, which attempts to clarify all such questions of definition, "A Green Hunter is a horse of any age that is in his first or second calendar year of showing in any classes at a regular member show requiring horses to jump." There is a totally different category called "Novice" where you can show your horse until doomsday if he doesn't work himself out of this classification. The "Novice" division is limited to those animals "which have not won three blue ribbons at Regular Member Shows in this division." In other words, "green" really means inexperienced in contrast to "Novice" which, for horse show purposes, indicates that a particular animal is not up to competing in top competition—or at least not yet. If he is, he will work his way out of the novice division speedily—sometimes at one show! By rule, in areas in which a green pony division exists, ponies may be "green" for one year only. Horses, both regionally and nationally, are permitted two green years. (Thus far, the green pony division is not considered for an A. H. S. A. high score award, although it is very popular in the areas in which it is held.) On the other hand, your horse or pony may be "Novice" all his life, or he may go out of "Novice" speedily, even while he is still "green."

The quotation from the A. H. S. A. rule book sounds deceptively simple and clear-cut, but unfortunately it doesn't work out exactly that way. Recounting the type of incident which resulted in recriminations and awkwardness for everyone concerned might point up the possibilities of "booboos" to avoid. A family with a talented fourteen-year-old daughter had become deeply involved with horses. Daughter was very tall, and had abandoned showing her brilliant hunter pony. Subsequently this family had come on an exceptionally able young thoroughbred who

Demonstrating good form on one of the gates of an outside hunter course.

schooled like a dream. About August of the year that they had bought him, a small recognized show was held near them that had a "Novice" division. Thus far, the few shows that they had taken the promising young horse to had been "unrecognized" which had no effect on his status. So now for a try in the novice division! He went well, ended the day Novice Champion, but because the novice division is not a "recognized division"—that is, fences are sub-standard height and it leads nowhere—the family did not think of the day as having anything to do with this horse's projected show ring career. The next year, this very able animal was brought out in the "First Year Green" division and was attracting quite a lot of favorable attention. About the middle of that year, such a big offer was made for this impressive young horse that the family was persuaded to sell him. A month or so later, with the horse standing somewhere around the top four of the "First Year Green" division nationally, someone made the observation that he had lost his status as a first year horse by showing over fences in the novice division of one small recognized show the previous year. The point was carried and a very unhappy situation followed.

Many similar slips could be cited, although this was one of the more dramatic—and traumatic! The point is that it is very important to thoroughly understand the rules of the game in which you are involved.

The novice division, which is designed as a sort of handicap section for animals that are not up to or ready for stiffer competition, has probably been the primary area of misunderstanding of status in the show ring, insofar as hunters are concerned. Regular divisions in regular member shows lead to a cumulative high score award annually. This obviously would be impossible in the case of the novice horse or pony, since as soon as that animal has won three blues at recognized shows he can no longer enter novice classes. Added to this, the fact that fences in the novice division are generally lower than the specified heights for regular divisions tends to create the impression in the mind of the owner that the horse has not really "shown over fences." The sad part of the picture is that, by definition, he has, and that one green year is shot!

Shows that are not members of A. H. S. A., but that are recognized by state organizations, may carry different rules, and interpretations of rules, in different parts of the country. Whenever there is any question of jeopardizing your horse's status in a way that might upset your future plans for showing him, contact the secretary of your particular state organization before you enter that show.

It is probably safe to make the statement that the "backyard" or "unrecognized" horse show (i.e., a show which is not a member of any state or national horse show organization) is the best place to gain needed experience for yourself or your mount.

Another good point to remember is that the word "novice" as applied to the rider will mean that the *individual* (not his mount) has or has not personally won three blue ribbons. Since it is only in horsemanship as opposed to performance that the rider is being judged, two totally different situations are being considered. The experienced rider who is by no means a "novice" will have every right to be on the novice horse or pony, in a performance division. On the other hand, the novice rider is best off on the veteran performer.

Officially, the rider, just as with the horse, is eligible for "Novice Horsemanship" classes until he or she has won three blue ribbons in horsemanship at recognized shows. In this country, the vast majority of horsemanship classes are designed for "junior riders" so that the *official* "novice" rider is the young person who has not reached his or her eighteenth birthday as of January one of that calendar year.

In spite of the fact that one might expect the individual who has moved far enough along the path of riding to be competing at shows to understand that in performance classes (i.e., "hunter ponies under saddle" or "junior working hunter stake," etc.) it is the *animal* whose performance is being judged, this does not always seem to be the case. Over and over again, you will hear the comment, "Polly got the large pony cham-

Rider being coached for hunt seat equitation demonstrates nice line from bit to elbow.

pionship," when in actuality what is meant is that her mount won that championship. Undoubtedly, the way Polly rode may have largely determined the fact, but it was the performance of the animal that was being judged. In horsemanship, of course, it is precisely the reverse.

Again, you will hear the comment along the horse show rail, "It really isn't fair that So-and-so should be competing at this little show. He got junior championship last winter at...." But here again, the person on the rail is confusing the two issues. It really wasn't the rider that "got junior champion" at the big show, but his mount. In this small unrecognized show where he was subject to the criticism, he was trying to give a very green young horse some experience. Pretty certainly, he would be ineligible for a "Novice Horsemanship Class," but that is a totally different story.

To consider horsemanship classes a little further, let's define a few more terms. A "Maiden Horsemanship Class" is a class for riders who have not won one blue ribbon in horsemanship in a recognized show. (A "Maiden Hunter Class" puts the same restriction on the horse; the *horse* may not have won one blue in performance. However, this type of class is not held too frequently, probably because there are other classes and divisions suited to the "maiden hunter.") Incidentally, a "Maiden" class, whether horsemanship or performance, has nothing at all to do with sex.

It is a "maiden" horsemanship class for boys as well as girls; it is a "maiden" hunter class for geldings as well as mares!

You may also see a class listed as "Limit Horsemanship." Such a class is open to riders who have not won six blue ribbons in horsemanship at recognized shows. The term "Limit" applied to the hunter indicates the same thing; the animal, in this case, may not have won six blue ribbons in performance to be eligible for a limit hunter class.

One other question of definition probably should be clarified at this point. This has to do with the "Junior Hunter." In certain types of competitions—for example, Arabian classes—junior refers to the animal. This would certainly seem to be the more logical definition of a junior horse. However, in the hunter divisions, a "junior hunter" is a horse of any age; junior refers to the rider. This could rightfully be called a sloppy definition since what we call a *junior* horse may not be a junior horse at all; he may be very much a senior citizen of the horse world, as far as his age is concerned. The "Junior Hunter" might, more accurately, be termed "Hunter for Junior Riders"—but this is a lot of words to incorporate along with the rest of the terminology. So, as with many expressions, it is simpler to accept the connotation that a particular term has taken on.

Making a fast review, you now know when you have a green horse and when he has lost his green status. You also know when you have a novice horse. You know in what situations maiden, novice and limit apply to the rider and when and how they apply to the horse or pony. And you understand that ambiguous expression that states that you are showing a "junior hunter!" ■

CHAPTER NINE

JUDGING HUNTER CLASSES — PERFORMANCE AND HORSEMANSHIP

The most mystifying aspect of the entire show hunter game is that of following the judging. It is here that the uninitiated exhibitor may find himself totally baffled. Even the very sophisticated show-goer may be at variance with the official results. For in judging hunter performance classes as well as hunter seat equitation, there is a great deal more to consider than simply the numerical penalty for major faults at fences. In a situation in which the individual judging the class must also consider the style over the fences, the way of going between fences, manners, the general impression that this animal creates as to being (to use the old-fashioned term) "an agreeable mount to hounds"—when you realize that he must try to reduce each of these aspects to the appropriate fraction of the whole, and come up with the right answer, it is not too surprising that there are differences of opinion.

Let's consider a few simple examples. Recently, a couple were watching their teenage daughter with the greatest excitement as she entered the ring. As you saw her make her entrance you pretty much knew what the round would be like. To begin with, the horse was thin, rough, high-headed and frightened. At the same time, the rider had managed to get her "revved" up to a point that she charged rather wildly into the ring, mouth open and nose pointing toward the sky. She was rapid and "rank" and obviously badly schooled in every respect. She did get around the course, making dreadful fences, jumping with dangling legs and caved-in back, but she didn't stop and nothing came down. From the point of view of the experienced show-goer, it was a terrible round. At the same time, the parents, standing with bated breath on the rail, turned to one another in great excitement, commenting, "She didn't touch any of the jumps, did she? She had a clean round, didn't she?" They then turned to meet and congratulate the exultant rider, who was happily awaiting a call at the end of the class and expecting a ribbon. The fact that their daughter didn't pin, in the minds of that family, meant that the judge was crooked, and was pinning his favorites, or that (again, unfairly to their minds) he was discriminating against their daughter because her clothes and the turnout of her mount were not as impressive as the others. Standing

A good athletic jump. Note excellent bascule and folding of front legs.

beside them on the rail, and hearing their resentful comments, and realizing that they had no grasp at all of what was expected in a good hunter round, you could not fail to feel distressed for them. At the same time, it was a bit difficult to start a casual conversation in which you explained to them some of the major faults of the round. With quite a lot of tact, sometimes the informed spectator can point out a few aspects that may start such a family on the path to understanding.

Another area in which the uninitiated become confused is in distinguishing performance classes from horsemanship classes. In performance classes, please remember, it is the *animal* that is being judged, not the rider. What the rider does is going to determine very largely what his mount does, but it is the performance of the mount that is being considered. Conversely, in any type of horsemanship class, it is the rider who is being judged—not the animal under him. Again, of course, the two are closely connected. For example, the judge has to assume that the rider would not have entered an equitation (horsemanship) class over fences if he did not have a mount that was capable of performing the requirements. So, faults of the horse do, in a sense, become faults of the rider. It is somewhat rare to find a rider "pinned on top" in a horsemanship class whose horse has refused a fence. The basis for this is the assumption that the rider would not have entered unless he had a mount capable of performing the class requirements. In the same sense, no one would enter a tennis match without an adequate racket or a golf tournament without suitable clubs! Therefore, had the rider made a good approach to the fence, there should have been no refusal. Once in a blue moon, you will see a rider pinned whose horse has had a major fault. But this would have to be the type of fault, as nearly as the judge can ascertain from watching, that could not have been anticipated, and hence prevented, by the rider. But the fault (let's say a refusal at the first fence) had best be corrected very skillfully and smoothly and the rest of the ride a real knockout!

It becomes difficult for spectators as well as parents to separate, mentally, the performance of the mount (in a performance class) from the performance and appearance of the rider. The endearing eight-year-old child who does a good job of taking her hunter pony over fences has the crowd with her—particularly if she and the pony look workmanlike and attractive. Sometimes the fact is overlooked, even by fairly knowledgeable spectators, that she did get one "short fence." But to be fair to the others in the ring, it is up to the judge to note this and mark the round accordingly.

In the case of judging horsemanship (where it is the skill of the rider that is to be considered), it becomes even more difficult to separate the wheat from the chaff. Let's suppose, for example, that Contestant A enters the ring on a gorgeous, beautifully moving, 17 hand Thoroughbred that has been schooled by a very clever professional. The groom has done a magnificent job of braiding and turning out this animal. The 3' 6" fences over which the horse will be ridden are child's play to him. Contestant A has an ideal rider's build. She is tall and slender and her clothes match her horse in quality. The tailor-made jacket and breeches and the custom-made boots enhance the air of quiet elegance that she creates as she enters the ring. She has an excellent round; it is smooth, unhurried and workmanlike, and she sits well.

Contestant B is her own groom, with only some rather inexpert parent assistance. She is neat and put her clothes on carefully, but obviously they were not made for her in England. Of medium height and slightly stocky in build, she looks just a little too large on her horse for each to set the other off to advantage. Her braid job is quite passable, her horse and her tack are clean, and the overall appearance could be termed adequate. Her mount is a bit on the "weedy" side; the little mare looks as though she might be a race track reject that came into her present owner's hands via a horse auction. She also gives the impression of being very edgy and ready to explode. It is obvious that only a very tactful ride will enable them to get around the course without mishap. Contestant B has an excellent round; she steadies her mount very softly where needed and completes the course with considerable brilliance.

Which of these two, who have been determined in the judge's mind as the top two, should be the winner? "Well," you may respond, "the way to decide this is to change horses. That should provide a conclusive answer." But will it, really?

Rider B comes back in on A's lovely horse; they have an excellent round. Rider A comes back on B's more temperamental mount. She looks very long legged on the small horse and doesn't seem terribly comfortable, physically, although her attitude is one of calm assurance. The horse she is on now will be much harder to change onto and get the feel of immediately than the other way around. The little mare did manage to "bomb" the last fence, taking a rail down. Which is the better rider? Has the matter definitely been settled? The judge must sign his card and turn it in. Actually, it has not really been completely determined, but in this class the judge will almost have to pin Contestant B over A. In this particular case, the disadvantages that B had initially turned out to be advantages.

There are so many variations as to what may happen, and so many ways in which two equally good judges will differ in opinions, that the spectator or exhibitor should do quite a lot of professional judging himself before he is too quick to criticize. Save those harsh words until you yourself have stood in the center of a ring some eight or ten hours on a hot dusty day, watching forty horses or ponies, one round close upon the other, go over eight fences, and provide an infallible decision in every case!

It is strongly recommended that anyone who plans to compete in any type of hunter competition should acquire a copy of the A.H.S.A. rule book, which will give a very detailed description of requirements and the manner in which hunter classes are to be judged. At the same time, many of the comments made in the rule book will not apply to the individual who will be showing mainly in what is termed "working classes." "Working Classes" or the "Working Division" refers to the division in which performance—and in judging hunters, this includes manners and way of going—and soundness count the full 100%. There is a totally different category of classes, or division, known as the "Conformation Division" in which performance accounts for 60% only; conformation makes up the other 40%. The chances are that the newcomer to showing need not concern himself too greatly about understanding the details of showing in this division. The conformation hunter is an expensive luxury. By the time the average individual has an entry for this division, he is not likely to need the help of this book!

And now, having made a general statement, I am forced to point out the inevitable exception! In the "Hunter Pony Division" and in the "Junior Hunter Division" it is permissible to have a mixed "Working" and

This pony's number has just been called to jog back in and line up. Those having the best rounds are called back to "jog for soundness" before ribbons are awarded.

"Conformation," division, all counting towards the same championship. But in this case, conformation will not account for more than 25% of the score; performance will account for 75%. About half the classes will be "working" and half "conformation," so you probably would enter the entire division, if you have a mount who is a good performer, even though he is not a "strip" animal. You will hope for an extra good trip, and you will hope too that the horse or pony who won the "Model" class is not lined up directly behind you! When each animal has completed his individual round over fences, the judge first calls them back "in the order of performance." That is to say, the number of the horse or pony which he feels had the best round is called first and so on through some eight or ten. Next, riders "stand up" their mounts to create the best possible effect, while the judge moves carefully around each, to arrive at a decision of relative merit on the basis of conformation. Here the order of line-up may change. So in a class in which conformation counts a certain percentage, the animal that was called in first does not necessarily end there; he may lose one or more notches in the final placing. Then there is another tense moment as each animal is "jogged for soundness." Each one is now trotted past the judge and scrutinized to be sure that there is no slight lameness. Finally, the judge signs his card and it is sent to the

Finalists from a large *under saddle* class wait to hear the results announced over the loud speaker.

announcer's stand—and the onlookers breathe a sigh of relief—or disappointment!

All this adds just a few more variables in the decision that the gentleman in the center is responsible for making—and making without any bona fide errors!

There are inevitably so many questions in the minds of those who do not know a great deal about the way hunter classes are judged, that we are including some sections from the 1971 A. H. S. A. Rule Book that you may find helpful. Better still, acquire or borrow one for yourself. You can't learn it all from any book, but it does help to have as complete a knowledge as you can acquire of the rules under which you are competing. The portions quoted here by no means comprise the complete section on hunters. Should you be unable to lay your hands on the book itself, these excerpts may help to give you a measure of understanding of certain technicalities in the matter of judging hunters. The following is from the 1971 A. H. S. A. Rule Book:

All horses must be serviceably sound. Any horse showing evidence of lameness, broken wind or impairment of vision shall be refused an award.

Performance:

An even hunting pace, manners, jumping style together with faults and way of moving over the course as well as when being jogged for soundness . . . (to be considered).

When the class is held in a ring the performance starts as the horse enters and ends when he leaves.

Judges shall penalize unsafe jumping and bad form over fences, whether touched or untouched.

In all classes over fences judges shall line up horses on merit of performance before considering conformation or soundness, including four more entries than the number of ribbons offered in Conformation Sections and two more entries in Working Section if there are sufficient entries without major faults.

NUMERICAL PENALTIES FOR TECHNICAL FAULTS AT FENCES
MAJOR FAULTS:

Knock-downs: An obstacle is considered knocked down when its height is lowered by horse or rider.

With any part of horse's body behind the stifle . . . . 4 faults
With any part of horse's body in front of the stifle . . . . 8 faults
Of standard or wing in jumping obstacle with any part of horse, rider or equipment. . . . . 8 faults
Of obstacle by touching a wing or post it shall count as a knock-down of obstacle with above penalties . . . . 8 faults
Placing any foot in Liverpool, ditch or water. . . . . 8 faults

Hind knock-downs, not the fault of bad jumping, shall not necessarily eliminate a horse from an award but should be scored against him in a comparative manner.

Circling once upon entering the ring and once upon leaving is permissible.

1st refusal, runout, bolting on course and extra circle . . . . 8 faults
2nd refusal, runout, bolting on course, extra circle . . . . . . 8 faults
3rd refusal, runout, bolting on course, extra circle . . . . . . 8 faults
Jumping an obstacle before it is reset . . . . Elimination
Bolting from ring . . . . Elimination
Failure to keep proper course . . . . Elimination
Jumping an obstacle not included in course . . . . Elimination
Horse and/or rider falling in competition. . . . . Elimination

A horse is considered to have fallen when shoulder and haunch on the same side touch the ground or the obstacle and the ground.

Light touches are not to be considered but may be scored according to scale below for reference in cases where elimination is difficult.

Touches with any part of horse's body behind the stifle . . . 1/2 fault
Touches with any part of horse's body in front of the stifle . 1 fault
Touches of standard or wing in jumping obstacle with any part of horse, rider or equipment. . . . . 1 fault ■

CONCLUSION

This booklet has been written to serve as a guide to individuals, already at home in the saddle, who may be unfamiliar with the particular conventions found in hunter circles. Obviously, it is not designed to *teach you to ride* and even less, to teach you to *school* your hunter. Learning the techniques of good riding normally should precede efforts to teach the animal. To accomplish either or both of the latter goals, you will need firsthand instruction. You will find, too, that you can greatly increase your general knowledge of riding techniques, and of schooling, by reading widely in these fields.

This volume should prove useful in explaining how you should look, and how your horse should look, in order to create an attractive appearance in the hunter show-ring, or in the hunt field. It also should serve as a ready source of reference as to how the horse moves. This knowledge will help you understand what the judge is looking for in the matter of good movement, good manners and general ability on the flat, or over fences.

Perhaps the greatest value that the book can provide will be to clarify a matter that is always puzzling to the uninformed—the mysteries of "hunter judging."

In any case, if you are moving into the field of riding and showing hunters, good fun, good sport, and good luck along the path! ■